TAKING THE NUMB OUT OF NUMBERS

Explaining and Presenting Financial Information with Confidence and Clarity

Dr. Stout –

Go Cards !

PRAISE FOR
TAKING THE NUMB OUT OF NUMBERS

"They say accounting existed even before written language and we know it is THE language of business. The challenge is when CPAs and finance professionals speak this language to non-financial people. Peter offers a practical guide for accounting and finance professionals to up their game in storytelling and presentation with lots of great examples, stories and tips. Use Peter's book to upgrade your 'self-ware' and make your presentations even better!"

Tom Hood, CPA
Executive Director & CEO of the Maryland Association of CPAs

"Imagine yourself captivating an audience with any financial presentation. That skillset is at your fingertips with Peter Margaritis's new book, *Taking the Numb Out of Numbers*. A must-read for any financial professional."

Hayden Williams, CPA
CFO at the Washington Society of CPAs

"If you're looking for practical advice on how to make compelling and interesting financial presentations, this is the one book you need to read and follow. Public speaking, even before audiences you know and with which you are comfortable, makes many people nervous — even fearful. Add in the complicating factor that your subject may be mind-numbing financial information that many don't understand under the best of circumstances and you have a double-whammy factor to overcome. The practical tips Pete Margaritis provides can make this challenge much easier to overcome and set you up for success.

The practical tips presented are common sense yet are often over-looked when it comes to financial presentations. By following the simple, practical guidance in *Taking the Numb Out of Numbers,* you can quickly move from nervous presenter to confident expert."

J. Clarke Price, FASAE, CAE
Retired CEO & President of the Ohio Society of CPAs

"*Taking the Numb out of Numbers* underscores the deep need for many financial people to be able to clearly explain the financial impact of decisions at every level. Peter Margaritis, CPA, is one of the very best at helping people understand an entire financial concept rather than seeing unrelated fragments. This new publication is a must-read for all financial people who strive to become influential leaders rather than traditional number-crunchers."

Jack Park, CPA, MBA, CSP

"If you're serious about getting better at public speaking, read this book. Each chapter is packed with ideas on how to incorporate the real secrets to great presentations: using stories, audience engagement and, of course, thinking on your feet. I wish I had learned these principles earlier in my accounting career!"

Kristen Rampe, CPA
Kristen Rampe Consulting

"The idea that my technical knowledge is akin to a foreign language was quite the "a-ha" moment for me. Peter provides an easy-to-follow approach to bridge the communication gap in an engaging and memorable way. The tools provided in this book will contribute significantly to my professional growth."

Ashley Matthews, CPA
Director of Tax, Crane Group Co.

"FINALLY, a lighthouse in the otherwise the foggy topic of good storytelling! Having read several books about storytelling, I have felt unfulfilled with respect to any actionable takeaways for creating great stories. YES, Peter reinforces the power of good storytelling AND provides the playbook for how to create great stories even when presenting the bland topic of financial information. A quality read for anyone looking to enhance their presentation skills!"

Byron Patrick, CPA
Managing Director, Network Alliance

"Peter unlocks the mystery behind how to find your voice to deliver advisory services with your clients in his book, *Take the Numb out of Numbers*. Not only is this book an easy and entertaining read, it draws the parallel between performing in front of an audience — whether it be as a comedian or any other entertainer — to human connection in client relationships. Peter reveals that the very same skills comedians practice every day can and do apply to the accounting profession. We can use his methodology to better uncover a client's pain points and create a story to tell them about their business so they better understand how to succeed."

Amy Vetter, CPA.CITP, CGMA
Keynote Speaker, Advisor and Author of *Integrative Advisory Services: Expanding Your Accounting Services Beyond the Cloud*

"I have trained finance professionals in presentation skills for more 30 years. Yet, the age-old statement that public speaking is one of the greatest human fears still exists. How do we break this paradigm? In *Taking the Numb Out of Numbers*, Peter Margaritis starts us off by focusing on improvisation. In today's business world, we must 'think on our feet,' actively listen to our colleagues and clients, and build on their statements and questions ('Yes! And ...'). Improvisation skills will help us 'take the numb out of numbers' and take the 'numb' out of a lot of other presentations as well. Thanks for challenging us, Peter!"

Robert Dean, CPA
Dean Learning & Talent Advisors LLC

"Peter takes 'the numb out of numbers' with practical tips and techniques, particularly around storytelling, that will elevate the effectiveness of any presentation. If you want to go from 'a bored room' to 'the board room,' then read this book now!"

Jennifer H. Elder, CPA, CMA, CIA, CFF, CGMA, MS
Consultant and Keynote Speaker

TAKING THE NUMB OUT OF NUMBERS

Explaining and Presenting
Financial Information with
Confidence and Clarity

PETER A. MARGARITIS CPA
The Accidental Accountant

With a foreword by Boyd E. Search, CAE,
CEO of the Georgia Society of CPAs

SILVER TREE
PUBLISHING

Editing by:
Claudia Trusty
Cathy Fyock
Karl Ahlrichs
Merle Heckman
Kate Colbert

Cover design by:
Tom Trusty and Courtney Hudson

Typesetting by:
Courtney Hudson

First edition, July 2018

ISBN: 978-1-948238-01-4

Library of Congress Control Number: 2018943068

Created in the United States of America

TAKING THE NUMB OUT OF NUMBERS

Explaining and Presenting
Financial Information with
Confidence and Clarity

PETER A. MARGARITIS CPA
The Accidental Accountant

With a foreword by Boyd E. Search, CAE,
CEO of the Georgia Society of CPAs

SILVER TREE
PUBLISHING

DEDICATION

I would like to dedicate this book to all the sharp financial professionals who deserve to be regarded as strategists, story-tellers, and game changers, and not just number crunchers. *Taking the Numb Out of Numbers* is for you.

TABLE OF CONTENTS

FOREWORD

I have long been teased by friends, family, and coworkers for being a chronic over-communicator, for which they get absolutely no argument from me. I have long defended my penchant for doing so to ensure that I am indeed connecting with people. "The single biggest problem in communication is the illusion that it has taken place ..." — those words from George Bernard Shaw have long formed the foundation of my personal communication style.

Communicating is hard because, as Peter Margaritis points out in this outstanding book, emotions trump logic. You will succeed or fail in connecting with your audience by how effectively you connect with their emotions. Far too often we see presenters (at conference sessions, in meetings, or just in casual pick-up meetings) use volumes of data and numbers to articulate a point. In so doing they lose their audience in a tidal wave of complexity. Numbers are not, in and of themselves, bad, but they rarely stand on their own — they provide support to the message you are trying to convey.

Nowhere can communication fail more quickly than in the world of translating data into information with vision and outcomes.

Storytelling has long been humanity's most effective way to share the past, inform the future, and build a culture of progress. Nowhere can communication fail more quickly than in the world of translating data into information with vision and outcomes. In building upon the art of improvisation, Peter uses the art of storytelling to help the reader construct their own storytelling method and style. The book is full of practical steps and tips that ultimately provide the reader with a recipe for ensuring successful connections. Peter's great love of connecting with people shines through.

Whether your communication style is undeveloped, underdeveloped, or you consider yourself a seasoned professional, this book will help build or reshape your perspective and approach in ways that will immediately pay dividends.

Boyd E. Search, CAE
CEO of the Georgia Society of CPAs

LETTER TO THE READER

Welcome to *Taking the Numb Out of Numbers*. When I have shared my book title with other accountants and financial professionals, many have said, "taking out the 'numb' just leaves you with 'ers.'" ERS, indeed. They are right, because when you take the numb out of numbers, that leaves you with Effective Relatable Stories (ERS). That is the essence of this book. There are a lot of variables that must be taken into consideration before you can become a more effective and engaging presenter of financial information, and this book will help you to become better.

It has been said that among the top 3 things that people intentionally avoid all their lives is public speaking. The fear is real, and it's common. Now imagine how much scarier such public speaking can be if you're facing the difficult task of delivering financial information to a group of folks who are not savvy when it comes to numbers or a 10-key or an Excel spreadsheet. Let's add on another layer of difficulty; you are an accountant and, like most accountants, you like details and tend to be a perfectionist. You don't like saying, "let me get back to you on that question" at any point.

I get it! Being a CPA, I realized that I had to get past those fears if I wanted my career to evolve from being a bean counter to truly helping organizations find solutions to their business challenges. That's why I wrote this book — because I suspect you have those very same fears, and because I'd like to help you get past them so you can become a better advisor to your clients and the organizations that you work for.

You will read in the following "About the Author" section that my background consists of standup and improv comedy. Let me make this perfectly clear up front: you don't need these two aspects to be engaging and impactful in your delivery. I share what I have learned from those two experiences to help you become a better presenter — a strong and engaging presenter of financial information.

You need to realize that you are cursed. That's right — cursed. You are "cursed with knowledge" and because of this, you have a hard time connecting with those who don't have your knowledge.

You can't change the numbers. However, you *can* change your delivery and bring those numbers to life.

You can't change the numbers. However, you *can* change your delivery and bring those numbers to life. Have you ever sat in a professional education course and been bored to tears? Have you tried to explain to a client changes in the tax law, only to see the deer-in-the-headlights look? Are you a treasurer for a not-for-profit board and your board report is more of a bored report?

The reason for reading this book can be summed up like this: It's time to change your mindset! Believe that strong communication skills are the most efficient and effective way to deliver your technical accounting knowledge. (You can also replace accounting with legal, engineering, or scientific. The principles on this book apply equally to the delivery of any kind of technical information.)

To become an effective communicator, you must capture your audience's attention, spark their imagination and offer information in a way they can understand and ultimately remember. The first step is to realize that the technical knowledge you possess is a foreign language to others. For example, you are a CPA and use the word *depreciation* to a non-CPA. They are immediately thinking about the value lost on a car when it is driven off the new car lot. All the while, you are thinking that depreciation is an allocation of an asset over time. Your audience lacks understanding in the way you communicate. Indeed, you speak a foreign language.

The way to begin to bridge the gap is comprehend that you speak a foreign language and find ways to translate accounting into plain English and make it memorable. To effectively do this, we need to find ways of putting complex information into a context that people can understand and remember. Storytelling and data visualization is the perfect way to bridge the gap.

Using stories, analogies, and metaphors helps you to deliver your message in a way that creates an emotional response for the receiver. Storytelling has educated, informed, and entertained us since the beginning of time and storytelling skills are a necessary business tool that allow us to enhance the way we visualize the data. Let me put it another way: facts, figures, and statistics do not drive decision-making, but stories that have an emotional component can drive your revenue higher.

Facts, figures, and statistics do not drive decision-making, but stories that have an emotional component can drive your revenue higher.

This book is designed to help financial professionals share their technical knowledge in a way that is more engaging to an audience. Engaging an audience is very important if you want them to act on your information. Have you ever sat in a lecture-style presentation being inundated with facts and figures, and, to make it worse, the presenter has a monotone voice? What are you thinking about during and after the presentation? Do you remember anything that was said? That is why engaging an audience is important.

Your audience can be a client in a one-on-one conversation or your audience might be 1,000 people packed into a ballroom wanting to hear what you have to say. An "audience" is anyone you are talking with (except for those people in your head!).

The key in connecting with your audience is that, "it's not about YOU, it's about your AUDIENCE." Put yourself in their shoes, view it from their perspective, and drive action. The sooner you realize that you are in the emotional transformation business and not the information delivery business, the more successful you and your organization will become.

The sooner you realize that you are in the emotional transformation business and not the information delivery business, the more successful you and your organization will become.

This is true whether you're giving a presentation at a Chamber of Commerce event or engaged in a conversation with a potential prospect. Surely, you have attended many networking events in your career. And if someone asks you, "tell me about your firm," you might respond with something like, "We are a full-service firm, with

8 partners, more than 100 professionals, and with three locations. We have been in the community for 50 years and provide award-winning service and solutions to our clients."

My response is *who cares?* You sound like your competition in providing the person facts and figures. Facts and figures don't drive decision making; emotions do, and stories are a way of delivering that message. A better answer to the question "tell me about your firm" might sound like this: "We're a unique firm in that what drives us is a focus on providing our employees with all the tools they need to be successful. For example, last year, we rolled out a new financial roadmap tool — kind of a visual planning tool — for our advisors, which they use to engage clients during initial meetings. As a result, our advisors have improved their contract closing rates and have doubled the amount of assets they manage. Our employees are doing a better job helping their clients enrich the lives of their own employees — and having more fun doing it."

Translating the foreign language of accounting and eliminating excessive amounts of facts and figures while replacing them with a story helps build respect, trust, and support between both parties. You now are the trusted business advisor.

About the Author

Let me take this moment and provide you with an overview of my background because it's relevant to what you're about to read, and because the only way we can connect in meaningful ways — reader and author — is for us to get to know one another.

I am a professional speaker and a member of the National Speakers Association. My speaking career began when I was 12 years old, bussing tables at a local restaurant. The customers were my audience, and I learned quickly that if I gave them the right amount of attention, and entertained them a bit too, I would get bigger tips.

I worked in restaurants until I was 24 years old (I know, it's a cliché — my Greek heritage destined me to at least a partial career in restaurants), followed by a job as a loan officer for a bank in Florida. As before, customers were still my audience. I focused on each person, talking with them in non-banking language, and I grew my business through referrals. Connecting with people was ingrained in my DNA.

At the age of 29, I left the balmy shores of Florida for the sun-soaked shores of ... wait for it ... Cleveland, Ohio, and enrolled in the Master of Accountancy program at Case Western Reserve University. This decision falls squarely on sage advice from my father, who always thought I would make a good CPA. I loved him, he loved me, and I took his advice (for once!). I graduated third in my class, then went to work for Price Waterhouse (now PricewaterhouseCoopers) and passed the CPA exam. Maybe dad was right; maybe I was a natural at this accounting thing.

If you think accounting is hard, try performing comedy in front of an audience.

During this time, to feed that part of me that yearned for an audience, I was also performing standup comedy and improv comedy. If you think accounting is hard, try performing comedy in front of an audience. It makes accounting look easy. My time on stage influenced my career as an educator and speaker, shaping how I now provide compelling presentations to my audiences.

But back to accounting. I have the highest respect for the accounting profession, but from the moment I stepped foot in the firm, I felt like I couldn't breathe. It was as if all the air had been sucked out of the office; it was downright stifling. I knew that I didn't fit in, at all. I grew up in gregarious environments and this was just the opposite. I felt like a fish out of water. It was so quiet you could hear a pin drop a mile away. As I sat at my desk, I could feel the sameness of each day coming my way. For the first time, my ability to interact and engage people was not a great asset.

Then it got even more difficult. CPAs must accumulate 40 hours a year of professional accounting education. Most of these courses are highly technical, full of PowerPoint slides with thousands of bullet points and featured a speaker who delivered every bit of information with a monotone voice: no expression, no eye contact, no life. It was dreadful, and I am sorry to say, still is in many cases. *Boring, boring, this was very boring!* But I endured each slow passing hour because I wanted to keep my license.

Eight years later, I started teaching accounting at a local university in Columbus, Ohio. In my case, the adage "Those who can, do. Those who can't, teach." is absolutely true. I was so bad at being a CPA that during a performance review, my boss asked me, "How in the hell did you ever become a CPA? You are an accidental accountant." That was the nicest thing she said to me in months! Years later, I named my business The Accidental Accountant and had the name trademarked.

As a teacher, however, I excelled. Many of my students thought I took the dry subject of accounting and made it fun. I drew upon my skills in standup and improv to make the learning environment fun and engaging. Let me share a quote from Mel Helitzer, who was a journalism professor at Ohio University, that motivated me. Mel said, "It's not what is taught at the university, it is what is caught. And if we can get students' mouths open with laughter, we can slip in a little food for thought."

The goal of any presentation is to exchange information in an engaging manner that increases the ability for the audience to retain and act of the information. A presentation can be a: meeting, discussion, teaching, proposing, influencing, motivating, persuading, speech, seminar, workshop, coaching, or any other interaction between you and others. As a teacher, I would experiment with different ways to make the foreign language of accounting relatable to my audience, my students.

During this time at the university, I recognized a real need for soft skills courses for the accounting profession, so I took that opportunity and began creating continuing education courses. Personally, I don't like the term *soft skills*, but when I use it I also say, "They may call them soft skills but they are very hard to master." Wouldn't you agree? The facial expressions in the classroom let me know that my students could relate to the term and the challenges it represents.

Let me fast forward to 2017 and writing this book. As a professional speaker and author who makes a living by giving speeches, facilitating seminars and workshops, creating an engaging experience is my goal. An engaging experience consist of, but is not limited to: asking questions, polling questions, using humor, storytelling, data visualization, role playing, question-reflection-sharing with the group, team building exercises, etc. When I develop and then deliver a presentation, I always reflect on my experiences taking those boring accounting continuing professional education courses. Then I do the exact opposite and I take risks. Writing this book is taking a risk. It's laying bare some of my stories for a broader audience — one full

of strangers I may never meet. It's trying to do what I do in the classroom in book form and hoping I don't fail. It's been an exciting and terrifying adventure.

I attribute a lot of my success to the knowledge that I have obtained from being a member of the National Speakers Association (NSA), both nationally and at the local chapter. Many of the best presenters in the world are members of NSA. If you want to be the best, you need to have access to the best, learn from the best, and watch the best.

The reason I am explaining this is because I want you to know that "CPA" doesn't define who I am. It is a part of me but not all. I have lived your life of long hours during busy season, sitting through CPE courses, and buried in an Excel spreadsheet. I understand your challenges and your opportunities. Those early years *before* I entered the accounting profession, however, are what make me unique to the profession. And I think that's a good thing!

My drive is to provide engaging, high-content and thought-provoking presentations where the audience can apply the tips and techniques I offer immediately. To achieve these goals, I had to learn a couple of things. First, make your presentation a conversation with your audience. The principles of improvisation have been of great value, and I will share those with my readers in this book. Second, bring your facts, figures, and data to life with the power of a story. Storytelling in the business world is compelling because it helps in decision making, along with inspiring others around you.

Making your presentation a compelling conversation takes hard work, and to achieve this you must change your mindset. You need to be determined to change your approach from merely an exchange of information (data dump) from one party to the next, to an engaging dialogue that includes facts and figures brought to life through the power of storytelling.

When you take shortcuts, you are thinking about yourself and not the audience. For example, you might think, "I don't have time to practice." Right there, you used the word *I* and made it about yourself. The better approach is, "I need to make the time to practice so the audience doesn't become bored during my presentation and begin playing Words with Friends."

WHAT'S IN THIS BOOK

This book is broken into three main sections:

- Section I: Making the Case for Storytelling
- Section II: Be Amazing and Engaging
- Section III: Case Studies

Let me give you an overview of what to expect as you make your way through the book.

Section I:
Making the Case for Storytelling

This section is where the major change in your mindset commences. That transformation begins with a discussion on why data visualization is not a synonym to data storytelling. Period! Next, time is invested in learning about how the brain functions and the way it reacts to boring facts and figures versus stories and analogies and they are so powerful. Now, that power can be used for good or evil and that propels the exploration of the dark side of storytelling. I'll raise your awareness about why it's critical that the facts and figures be congruent with the story being told. The goal of this section is to show how business storytelling is the best way for you to connect with people in meaningful ways.

Section II:
Be Amazing and Engaging

This section is about everything you need to know before and during your presentation. This is broken down into four main themes:

- Getting past your fear of public speaking
- Knowing your audience
- Preparation and delivery
- Being authentic

Section III:
Case Studies

There are four case studies to help you visualize the techniques that are described in this book. These case studies were developed from current clients, past presentations, and observations.

In a Nutshell

This book will help you take your technical accounting knowledge, combine it with new techniques, and become a more effective and engaging communicator, which is critical for your future development.

In 2011, the AICPA issued the Horizons 2025 report,[1] which was a grassroots effort to understand the evolving role of the CPA

---

1   AICPA, Horizons 2025 Report, https://www.aicpa.org/Research/CPAHorizons2025/DownloadableDocuments/cpa-horizons-report-web.pdf.

profession as it moves toward the year 2025. This report identified six core competencies that CPAs must possess and/or develop during this time. In those core competencies are: communication skills, leadership skills, critical thinking and problem-solving skills, anticipating and serving evolving needs, synthesizing intelligence to insight, and integration and collaboration.

The very first competency addressed is communication skills in an effort to ensure that "CPAs are able to effectively exchange reliable and meaningful information, using appropriate context and interpersonal skills."[2] This book, I believe, goes a long way toward addressing this critical core competency.

Since the publication of the AICPA Horizons 2025 report, the stakes have been raised even higher due to rapid improvements in technology. Artificial intelligence has already entered the profession in the audit function and tax practices. IBM's Watson is now doing a lot of our number crunching and leaving us with the information needed to help organizations to grow. We are seeing artificial intelligence in the major accounting firms, and it has cascaded itself throughout public accounting firms and finance departments in large organizations.

The Maryland Association of Certified Public Accountants, Inc., and the Business Learning Institute, in 2017, wrote two white papers titled *Human Work in the Age of Machines: Five Steps for Building a Future Ready Finance Team* and *Human Work in the Age of Machines:*

---

2   *Ibid.*

Five Steps for Building a Future Ready Accounting Firm.[3] Are you future ready?

Now is the time to begin taking inventory of your current interpersonal skill set to determine what skills are missing so you can develop a plan to develop those skills. One of the top five fears that people have is public speaking and if you're reading this book it may be one of yours. As I stated earlier, the audience can be the recipient of a one-on-one conversation a room of 1,000 people listening to a presentation. This book will help you become a better public speaker if you use the techniques outlined and commit to practicing them.

Effective communication is complex and takes time to master. One CFO told me that she is multilingual: she knows the language of engineering, the language of human resources, the language of IT, and the language of accounting. She translates all of these into plain English when communicating with the CEO, the Board of Directors, the bank, and other stakeholders. Remember, accounting is a foreign language.

The accounting profession has provided so many with opportunities that I would have never imagined. Albeit, I am The Accidental Accountant, but I have found ways to take my knowledge and experiences and find my niche in this profession. Dad, it was good advice after all.

---

3   The Maryland Association of Certified Public Accountants, Inc., and the Business Learning Institute, 2017, *Human Work in the Age of Machines: Five Steps for Building a Future Ready Finance Team and Human Work in the Age of Machines: Five Steps for Building a Future Ready Accounting Firm,* https://www.macpa.org/new-e-books-offer-steps-toward-future-readiness-for-cpas-finance-professionals/.

Chapter 1

SUCCESSFUL PRESENTATIONS START WITH IMPROV

> *"The freedom to fail is so important."*
>
> — Anne Conderacci, The Second City Alumni

The principles of improvisation start with the two of the most powerful words in the English language: Yes, and. The philosophy of "Yes, and ..." supports creating conversations where people can come to an agreement without always agreeing. We can acknowledge the other's position ("Yes!") and build upon it or take the idea in a different direction ("And I also think it's interesting that ..."). It is about putting yourself in the other person's shoes and empathizing with their situation. This same philosophy applies when you develop a presentation. Think about it — how many times have you sat through a totally boring presentation, totally disengaged, while the presenter droned on, oblivious to the audience's lack of participation? More than you can count, I bet. The presenter was not connected to the audience's feelings or reactions; he or she wasn't displaying any empathy for the audience.

Just to be clear, I define the term presentation to be a speaking event in front an audience, no matter the size. This could be a speech at a Rotary Club, presenting at a lunch-and-learn or the board of directors, facilitating a meeting, even having a one-on-one conversation with a colleague. The philosophy of "Yes, and ..." teaches you to empathize with the audience, to become acutely aware of their reactions. Through "Yes, and ...," you become an engaging and entertaining presenter who connects with the audience on multiple levels.

For the philosophy of "Yes, and ..." to be effective, you need to create a solid foundation built upon respect, trust, and support.

Let's start with respect. You must show the audience that you respect them through your body language, your appearance, and your tone of your voice. If you're demonstrating poor body language, dressed unprofessionally, and have a harsh tone in your voice, what do you think the audience is thinking about you? You have just put a wall between you and them.

Trust is something that you earn. You earn the audience's trust by being honest and open with them. Trust is communicated through our body language, primarily with our hands and arms. When your arms are extended away from your body and your palms are pointed upward, you are communicating to the audience that you are truthful and honest. This is referred to as the "trust plane," and is a very important tool for every speaker.

Support is demonstrated in a couple of very different ways. One way is to remember that your audience doesn't want to see you fail. When you show them respect and trust, they will support you.

Remember that your audience doesn't want to see you fail. When you show them respect and trust, they will support you.

Listening and Focusing

Now that we have the foundation laid out, the next two principles of improvisation — listening and focusing — are the most important to master, and the most difficult to achieve. Even trickier, you must execute them simultaneously.

There are two types of listeners: those who listen to respond and those who listen to understand.

There are two types of listeners: those who listen to respond and those who listen to understand. Listening to respond is when we impatiently wait for our turn to talk or interrupt the other person so we can talk *at* them. When we listen to respond, we have an agenda that we want to achieve, and we will achieve that agenda no matter what the other person is saying. When we listen to respond, we discount their thoughts and ideas (whether or not we consciously mean to), and that leaves our audience likely to believe we don't respect them or their position.

Diametrically opposed to that, listening to understand (or active listening) happens when we park our agenda and actually listen to the other person without getting ahead or drifting off. Listening to understand creates a dialogue of questions and answers and, by doing so, allows us to gain a better understanding of the audience's wants and needs.

Listening to understand is about focus. Focusing requires us to eliminate all distractions during our conversation. These distractions can be internal distractions, like personal biases, or external distractions, like like problems with technology or noises that threaten to disrupt the communication. It is very difficult to maintain intense focus 24/7/365. However, there are times that we need to be focused, present, and in the moment, especially when we are presenting important information. It's the first step in being able to better understand and assess the situation at hand.

When you are in front of an audience, you can maintain your focus by using what you see and hear to interpret the body language of the audience. Your audience's body language tells you if they're engaged in conversation, bored to death, or if you have said something to distract or offend them. I have been an audience member during some of those boring accounting-related topics, and the rest of the audience was clearly bored out of their minds, too. However, the presenter ignored the signals we sent and didn't modify their presentation to offer a story, or ask questions, or even give the audience break. They just keep plowing through the data, completely anesthetizing the audience!

Adaptability

The last principle of improvisation is adaptability. The ability to adapt to any situation is a must because no matter how well-planned or practiced your presentation is, unexpected events can happen. Maybe your computer freezes, there could be a sudden power outage, a waiter drops a tray of glasses, an audience member gets sick, or your time is cut in half at the last minute. When you fully employ the principles of improvisation, you can adapt to any situation, no matter what. Adaptability is really a key ingredient to your success as a presenter.

The ability to adapt to any situation is a must because no matter how well-planned or practiced your presentation is, unexpected events can happen.

Recently, I was discussing an upcoming presentation with a client and asked how much time my presentation was allotted. He replied "one hour," but he had this funny look on his face, so I had to ask why the strange expression. He shared with me that the presenter the month before had a presentation that he had developed to last 90 minutes, and when told of the one-hour limit, the speaker didn't modify his presentation to meet the client's expectations. Well, he just violated every principle of improvisation and eliminated the likelihood of that client asking him to speak again. On top of that, if anybody calls my client to ask about that presenter, he is guaranteed a poor reference.

Improvisation is always about remembering that your audience comes before yourself. "Yes, and … " can help you empathize with them, really listen to them, focus on what they need, and adapt to any situation you may face. The principles of improvisation will help you connect with and engage every audience so each presentation is a success. Oh, one more thing: please, always wear comfortable shoes!

Chapter 2

WHAT STANDUP COMEDY TEACHES US ABOUT PUBLIC SPEAKING

> *"Humor can give you the edge you are looking for."*
>
> — Jeffrey Gitomer

Becoming a great presenter takes effort and commitment. While there are several methods that can improve your performance, the more practice you have in front of a real audience the more improvement you will make. I am going to share with you what I learned in performing standup comedy and how it helped guide me to become a professional speaker.

Back in the late 80s and through most of the 90s, I performed in comedy clubs, and I learned a lot about presenting to audiences. Full disclosure: I was never a professional comedian who traveled the country and earned a living from making people laugh. However, standing in front of an intoxicated audience, telling jokes and hoping for laughs, and getting my fair share of crickets, provided a great training ground. I suggest standup for anyone who wants to become a better speaker, professional or not. Standup comedy helps you learn to read an audience, learn about practice and preparation, write tighter (i.e., achieve word economy), take risks, and look for stories that make you show the authentic you.

On my podcast, *Improv Is No Joke*, I have interviewed several professional comedians, and I asked each of them what standup comedy taught them about being a better presenter. Here are excerpts from my interviews with Dan Swartwout, Rik Roberts, and Judy Carter, all professional speakers and comedians.

Dan Swartwout

Dan Swartwout is a professional touring comedian who is also an attorney and a member of the City of Powell (Ohio) City Council. Here are some of the insights he shared with me:

- *"[Standup has taught me] the ability to read an audience, the ability to measure my performance based on the audience's reactions and expectations, and I think a lot of those skills are translatable to many different types of performances and speaking engagements."*

- *"The key between a good speaker and a great speaker is the great speaker and the good speaker are both prepared and ready, and on top of what it is they're going to do. The great speaker, however, doesn't appear to be over-prepared. It seems they're just talking to you, even though they know exactly what they're going to say, what they're going to do, and how they're going to do it to the audience."*

- *"Let's say you're doing a presentation in front of accountants and you're in the middle of your presentation and somebody drops a tray full of glasses, and the glasses shatter everywhere. I mean that's something that, if it unnerved you, it could throw off your entire presentation. Keep connecting with your audience regardless of what might happen. Anytime you get in front of a group of people and talk, there is always room for error."*

Rik Roberts

Rik Roberts provides clean comedy and creative keynote presentations. Rik also provides excellent comedy writing and performing skills in his School of Laughs, in person and online. His comedy classes will help anyone who wants to add more humor to their writing. Some of Rik's thoughts about the connection between comedy and presentation skills include:

- *"Doing the comedy clubs was like going through all four years of college, and you get an education and you get that experience level from having faced every type of audience and tough crowd. Comedy College! Just go out there and experience it and take those lessons to the corporate speaking world."*

- *"Comedy is an art and sculpting is an art. In comedy, if they gave us 30 pounds of words, we would try to use all 30 pounds. A sculptor would take those 30 pounds of clay and chisel away what doesn't need to be there. Amateur comics don't. They try to use all 30 pounds of words. But a professional will try to get that down to the bare minimum [like the sculptor does]. An artist removes things so that you can see the beauty of the art, whereas a laborious person would just use everything to show you that they can do it."*

- *"When I deliver speeches, even though there's plenty of humorous points in there and lots of funny stories and jokes, when I'm delivering the contents of the material (and it's taken me awhile to learn this), I need to slow down and hear it as I'm saying it, as if it's the first time I'm saying it, because that's how the audience is receiving it."*

Judy Carter

Judy Carter is a keynote speaker, the incredible author of *The Message of You* and *The Comedy Bible*, and an effective coach. She is also retired from an impressive career as a standup comedienne. Here are some excerpts from our interview:

- *"We all have this attitude that our life is absolute, random and chaotic, and in reading my book ..., people find that it's not random, it's not chaotic. That you actually have a message in your life and every day you're living that message, and you have something in your stories and what you've gone through that, if you share, can really help other people and create a ripple effect of inspiration."*

- *"[Consider] what happened today and find one moment in the day where something upset you, because we find that when things upset you they kind of hook into something that happened before, usually in your childhood, and from that we can glean a message. And we don't have to wait for dramatic things to happen to us. Extraordinary events are happening every day, and when we can capture that, it helps find exactly what is our legacy."*

- *"What is therapy except knowledge about yourself? Understanding what motivates you, what rules you, because that's power. I mean people go to therapy. But a lot of people want self-knowledge, so they can use it to be an influencer in the world and understand, so they're able to answer that question: what do I want to do?"*

This is great advice from very seasoned comedians on what they have learned from standup comedy, and it's advice I hope you'll internalize and apply to your own life and work. Here's a challenge for you: put yourself out there and try standup, even in a really casual way. Write seven jokes and go to an open mic night to try your material. Before you venture out for the first time, I have a very important tip — do your homework. Find out how many minutes of mic time you will have, then practice your routine with a stopwatch. If you go over your time limit, you probably will not get any more stage time at that venue for a while. On performance day, your goal is to take mental notes of everything you observe while on and off stage. Watch and listen to the other amateurs, watch the audience reactions, stay in the moment. After your set, write down your observations and come back better prepared the next week.

If standup is too far outside your comfort zone, then I would suggest joining a Toastmasters International club. This is a great place to begin to work on the craft of public speaking. I got my start at a local Toastmasters club, as did many of my National Speakers Association colleagues.

➤ You can listen to my full interviews with Dan, Rik, and Judy on my podcast, *Improv Is No Joke*, by going to my website www.PeterMargaritis.com and selecting the *Improv Is No Joke* podcast icon on the home page.

Section I

MAKING THE CASE FOR STORYTELLING

Chapter 3

DATA STORYTELLING VS. DATA VISUALIZATION

> *"Stories are just data with a soul."*
>
> — Brene Brown, TEDx Houston 2010

Lately, the term *data visualization* is used in the same context as *data storytelling*, which is incorrect. Data visualization is presenting data as a picture or in a graph. It assists in helping the audience to understand complex concepts more easily and helps them retain the information longer through pictures. Data visualization is an aid in your story.

The key word in the last sentence is that it is an *aid* in your story. When you use pictures and graphs to help deliver your story, this aids in helping the audience to comprehend and retain the message you are delivering. But the visual aid isn't the whole story.

A recent *Forbes* article, "He Turned Data Storytelling Success into Data Storytelling Failure. Here's What Went Wrong," talks about the difference between data visualization and data storytelling.[1] The author, Meta S. Brown, crafts the argument that the two concepts are not the same by stating that "data storytelling is a way to share facts in the form that your listener understands, appreciates and remembers best — the story." A story is about a person, or a goal, or a challenge and within this is the emotion that surrounds the event. Data stories have all the same components as everyday stories, but they contain the data to back it up and that data must be congruent to be credible.

In visualizing your data in a PowerPoint presentation, for example, the goal is to create something that's easy on the eyes of your audience and doesn't confuse them. Putting an Excel spreadsheet with 21 columns and 26 rows into a PowerPoint slide does not constitute a graph and is not easy on the audience's eyes. If you have to squint your eyes to see the information, then find a way to eliminate the unnecessary data and then use a larger font. If not, you are giving the audience permission to check their email.

I have a consulting client who specialized in business valuations and forensic accounting. He had an upcoming conference presentation and wanted my opinion on his presentation. He has delivered his business valuation presentation several times and commented that during his presentation, he could tell that he was losing the audience, especially at the very complex concepts supported by graphs.

After reviewing his presentation, I expressed to him that I liked that he was using graphs to help explain these complex concepts. However, there was too much data jammed into a single graph, and

---

1   Brown, Meta S., "He Turned Data Storytelling Success into Data Storytelling Failure; Here's What Went Wrong," *Forbes*, January 30, 2018, https://www.forbes.com/sites/metabrown/2018/01/30/he-turned-data-storytelling-success-into-data-storytelling-failure-heres-what-went-wrong/#2c1a106748a5.

in one graph, there were seven arrows scattered in a data-jammed graph. One last thing, the font size was too small which created another distraction. My suggestion was to eliminate any unnecessary information from the data and only put what is pertinent and not repetitive. Also, I suggested that he break up the information into separate slides with only one arrow (instead of seven) per slide and where the discussion or story could be more focused.

Remember Rik Roberts, the clean comedian? He was speaking at a conference and posted on his Facebook page a picture that speaks to this issue. The photo was from the back of the room; the screen was filled with a spreadsheet jammed with data and the presenter said, "I know this slide is hard to see, but there is a lot of information to see." Rik posted that he almost laughed out loud. I posted, "Is the person presenting an accountant?" He replied, "How did you know?"

To convey your thoughts, ideas, and action items wrapped around facts, figures, and statistics, remember to find the person, circumstance, or goal first. Explore the reasons surrounding the situation in telling the story and support your story with the graphs and pictures and be able to connect with your audience which will help in clarifying any confusion that could impede full understanding. That is the main idea of this book and the chapters that follow.

To convey your thoughts, ideas, and action items wrapped around facts, figures, and statistics, remember to find the person, circumstance, or goal first.

Takeaways

- Data visualization is a great aid to data storytelling.

- A story is about a person, or a goal, or a challenge and within this is the emotion that surrounds the story.

- Putting an Excel spreadsheet with 21 columns and 26 rows into a PowerPoint slide does not constitute a graph.

Chapter 4

WHY STORYTELLING IS POWERFUL

> *"The art of storytelling can be used to drive change."*
>
> — Richard Branson

We all love a good story and appreciate a good storyteller. Powerful stories evoke emotion, can motivate and inspire us, and can make us smile and make us cry. Stories help us in making decisions because of the emotions they tend to evoke.

Stories help us in making decisions because of the emotions they tend to evoke.

Billionaire entrepreneur Richard Branson said, "The art of storytelling can be used to drive change." I agree and will add that the way we succeed in driving change is by motivating and inspiring people. Do we inspire and motivate change with a data dump of facts and figures on a PowerPoint slide? No. That type of presentation just creates a lullaby that too often puts the audience asleep. According to Carmen Gallo, author of *The Storyteller's Secret: From TED Speakers to Business Legends, Why Some Ideas Catch On and Others Don't,* "If people aren't entertained, they stop listening and go to sleep not unlike what happens in millions of business presentations given every day."[5]

In the book, Gallo describes the power of storytelling by referencing a quote from Princeton University neuroscientist Uri Hanson, which states, "Those who have mastered the skill of storytelling can have an outsized influence over others." He conveys that when we tell stories, we begin to insert ideas, thoughts, and emotions into the person's brain. Storytelling is a powerful tool in helping to turn ideas into action.[6]

The only way to understand the power of this tool is to understand how the brain functions when hearing a story. Hearing a moving story releases the chemical dopamine in our system. That's right, the same chemical that can get us addicted to drugs, alcohol, and gambling. According to John Medina, author of *Brain Rules,* "When your brain detects an emotionally charged event, your amygdala releases dopamine in to your system. Dopamine aids memory and information processing. You can think of it like a Post-It note that reads 'Remember this.'"[7]

In Simon Sinek's Ted Talk "How Great Leaders Inspire," he describes the golden circle: Why, How, What. We all know what we do and how we do it, but do we know *why* we are doing it? He ties this concept

---

5   Gallo, Carmine, *The Storyteller's Secret: From TED Speakers to Business Legends, Why Some Ideas Catch On and Others Don't,* (St. Martins Press, New York, 2016), 3.

6   *Ibid.*

7   Medina, John, *Brain Rules: 12 Principles for Surviving and Thriving at Work, Home and School,* (Pear Press, Seattle, WA, 2014) 112.

back to the brain and explains the brain slightly differently than John Medina, although the message remains the same.

Sinek describes our brain as having three major components which align themselves with the golden circle concept. First, the neocortex is responsible for our analytical thought and language, and corresponds with the "what level" in the golden circle. Our limbic brains (the other two components) are responsible for our feelings, our human behavior, and our decision making. This relates to the "how" and "why" components of the golden circle.

Sinek goes on to argue that when we communicate starting with the "why," then "how," and then end with "what," we can drive behavior because we are speaking to the limbic parts of the brain that drive human behavior and decision-making. However, most people communicate in the opposite manner, starting with "what they do" and then "how they do it" but never tell "why." By doing so, they are only communicating facts, data, and statistics and never applying any emotion, which drives decision making.

In other words, emotion trumps logic, every time. This is why stories are so powerful. They evoke emotion, and emotion drives behavior. Marketing executives understand this and if you don't believe me, watch most commercials. Budweiser commercials, particularly their Super Bowl ads, are a case in point. In my favorite Budweiser commercials, the marketers use Clydesdales horses and Dalmatian dogs to tell a story. Go to YouTube and watch *Budweiser Clydesdale Getting Trained by Bud Dalmatian, Separated at Birth,* and *Budweiser Clydesdale Fetching a Stick.* You will see and feel the emotion while watching these commercials. Reflect on what you are feeling and think about ways you can do the same in your business.

Once we accept the fact that "emotion outperforms logic" and begin to craft our business presentations in the same manner, the more likely we will be able to inspire and motive people to action. That is exactly what great leaders and organizations do.

Takeaways

- "When your brain detects emotion, it releases dopamine. Dopamine aids memory and information processing. It like a Post-It note that reads "remember this.""

- Storytelling is a powerful tool in helping you to turn ideas into action.

- Emotion trumps logic, and ultimately drives decision making.

Chapter 5

STORYTELLING AND OUR BRAINS

> *"We don't pay attention to boring things."*
>
> — John Medina

Wrapping a good message inside a great story helps you to connect with your audience, engage them in the material, and ensure they can retain what they heard. For instance, most TED Talks work because the speakers are using their personal stories to help deliver their messages. Every TED Talk shares a common trait: they contain emotional components that grab our attention from the first sentence to the last. They make it nearly impossible to stop watching. You pay attention, and you stay connected because you want to see how the story ends.

Whether the presenter uses humor, fear, empathy, or tragedy, TED Talks are the direct opposite of most business presentations you get at a conference, seminar, or boardroom. I call those "sleeping-pill presentations" — data packed, mind-numbing PowerPoint presentations that challenge every person in the audience to remain awake. Becoming engaged in the topic is nearly impossible.

According to John Medina, author of the book *Brain Rules*, "The brain doesn't pay attention to boring things."[8] He is right. The better you are at capturing the attention of your audience, the more they will learn, and isn't that the overall goal? Consider your own behavior. When sitting through a sleeping-pill presentation, do you pay attention to the speaker or, maybe, your smartphone?

I have a brain and I am an armchair expert on the brain, but I do rely on a true brain *expert*: John Medina's research to help explain how storytelling affects our brains. According to Medina, "emotions get our attention."[9] When we pay attention, we capture and retain details.

Here's an example from my past that probably resonates with you. I was attending a Stephen Covey presentation on September 11, 2001. I left the ballroom to use the restroom and walked by a group of people huddled around a small TV and overheard them saying, "a plane just crashed into one of the Twin Towers." As of the writing of this book, that was nearly 17 years ago. I can't tell you what I was doing 17 hours ago. Medina was right about emotionally charged events! That entire day and weeks later were packed with so much emotion that many of us will never forget. How could we possibly?

During an emotionally charged event, we feel fear, anger, sadness, joy, disgust, surprise, and other automatic responses. During my presentations, I tend to focus on one emotion: surprise. One way of looking at the emotion of surprise is including something unexpected, like humor. I will discuss this in greater detail later in the book, but humor goes a long way in helping to keep the attention of an audience.

---

8   Medina, John, *Brain Rules: 12 Principles for Surviving and Thriving at Work, Home and School*, (Pear Press, Seattle, WA, 2014) 112.

9   *Ibid.*

Jeffrey Gitomer, who is an author, professional speaker, and business trainer, has been quoted saying, "The end of laughter is followed by the height of listening." Think back to your college days. What class did you enjoy attending? Why? It was probably because the teacher used stories and humor to capture your attention and get you involved as an active listener. When I was working on my Master's Degree in Accountancy, I had to take a corporate income tax class. I was dreading that semester because, to me, corporate income tax sounded like the pinnacle of boredom. It turns out, however, that class was the one I always looked forward to and enjoyed the most. The reason was Professor David Jaeger. He made tax fun, which is a feat in and of itself! He told stories, and he used humor to explain the complexities of the tax code. He always wore a suit and tie, and on most days, he would wear his "boxer shorts" tie. There are many ways to deliver humor.

Do I remember everything I learned in his class? Of course not! That was more than 20 years ago. However, I do remember his name, I do remember his tie, and I do remember that I enjoyed his class. Very different from my memories of my auditing course. I don't remember who taught the class; I don't remember anything about the class. I do remember that when I passed the CPA exam, the section that I passed first was taxation and the part I struggled with, and finally passed, was auditing. Coincidence? I doubt it.

Apparently, I had a lot of Post-It notes in my brain about taxation and very few about auditing. Later in this chapter, I will discuss how to craft a story but for now, remember to include emotionally charged stories in your presentations. Help your audience and their brains pay attention to you and what you are saying. Your stories will become the Post-It notes they can recall just when they need them.

Takeaways

- Avoid "sleeping-pill presentations" — data packed, mind-numbing PowerPoint presentations that challenge every person in the audience to remain awake. Becoming engaged in the topic is nearly impossible.

- Emotions get your attention. When we pay attention, we capture and retain details.

- The end of laughter is followed by the height of listening.

Chapter 6

SCOPE OF A STORY

"Stories have a unique power to move people's hearts."

— Peter Guber, author of *Tell to Win*

Now that we know the impact a story has on our brains, let's begin to examine the scope of a story. All stories have the same basic structure: they have a beginning, a middle, and an end. Each layer of the structure serves a specific role in advancing the story.

The beginning of the story is where the main characters and the intentions of each are introduced and the setting of the story is disclosed. Put another way, when you are using your experiences with clients, associates, and your family to make a point, take time to gather the necessary details to set the beginning of your story.

The mood and tone are also established during this time frame. The beginning of a story usually constitutes 10% to 20% of the full story. Any less and you will leave out key details, any more and you may lose the interest of your audience. Once the characters, mood and tone are revealed, the main conflict (or pivot) is introduced and the action transitions to the middle or body of the story. The challenge of the beginning is to be detailed yet succinct.

The middle is where the tension of the main conflict begins and escalates to its completion. This tension is built on actions and dialogue that let the audience connect with the characters and the situation surrounding them. There may be suspense, romance, fear, loathing, or some other emotion that gets the audience engaged and involved, even committed, to the story. It is during this part that we begin to see the characters change or evolve as they deal with the conflict. The middle is the bulk of the action and will make up 60% to 80% of the story.

The end of the story is where the conflict has been resolved and any loose ends are tied up in a nice bow. The tension has been eliminated and the story concludes.

Many have described this structure as the story arc, which looks like an inverted check mark. The story is introduced, tension builds to the point of resolution and then quickly moves to completion.

Now that we have established the structure of a typical story, let's explore the five components of a good story: time, place, characters, conflict, and resolution.

Time and place: This is your starting point and establishes a point of reference in the audience's mind. To help your audience connect with your story from the very beginning, be specific about when and where the story happens.

Characters: The characters will always include a protagonist and an antagonist, or, as I like to refer to them, a hero and a villain. Additional characters give dimension to your story.

Conflict: The villain creates a problem for the hero, a struggle that will continue to build until the story's climax. This conflict evokes an emotional response in the characters and with the audience, and it is a critical component of every good story. It is what keeps you on the edge of your seat when watching a movie or reading a book.

Resolution: The conflict has been resolved and the story ends.

The time, place, and characters are established at the beginning of the story, then the conflict occurs as the transition to the middle. The middle comprises a variety of events, which escalate the conflict and increase the tension. Obviously, when the conflict has been resolved, the story has come to its logical end.

Dissecting a story into its basic structure and then identifying the five components becomes easier with practice. Watch a movie, sitcom, or a TED talk and begin to break each down into its components and look for those emotionally charged moments. Just like anything, the more you practice, the better you will get. Understanding how to *identify* the key elements of a great story is the first step to helping you *craft* great stories so you can deliver more engaging presentations.

Next up in this book? We will spend time finding and crafting our story through my storytelling method of I.M.P.R.O.V.

Takeaways

- The beginning of the story is where the main characters and the setting are introduced, along with the intentions of each character.
- The middle is where the tension of the main conflict begins and escalates to its completion.

- The end of the story is where the conflict has been resolved and any loose ends are tied up in a nice bow.

Chapter 7

FINDING THE STORY

> *"Life has meaning only in the struggle."*
>
> — Stevie Wonder

Some of the great storytellers of our time are Walt Disney, Sheryl Sandberg, Bruce Springsteen, and Steve Jobs. What do they all have in common? Their stories follow the flow as described in the previous chapter.

There are stories all around us. We just need to take the time to recognize them and write them down. As I mentioned in the in Chapter 6, all stories have a hero and a villain. Think about it this way — as a financial professional, you help solve your client's (external and internal client's) problems. You (your company, your team, etc.) are the hero because you slay the villain by solving the problem. When you think a hero/villain in this manner, you will recognize that stories are all around you.

There are stories all around us. We just need to take the time to recognize them and write them down.

In the development of the story, let's use a system (template) in helping us to create a story that will be impactful. Taking everything that I have learned, I developed my own method of storytelling and it is the acronym I.M.P.R.O.V. Go figure, right?! Let's explore.

I – Identify

M – Mining

P – Pivot

R – Raise

O – Out

V – Victory

Identify and **Mining** are used in finding your story and developing the beginning of your story. The **Pivot**, **Out**, and **Victory** are used in crafting your story and developing the middle and end of your story, which is discussed in the next section.

Identify

This is where you need to identify things that you are trying to solve, challenges that you are facing, or things that started off well but then went sideways. These can be anything from very large events like a heart attack to something as small as a papercut. Sit down in front of your computer, or at your desk with a pen and pad of paper, and take 10 minutes and write down situations in your business life when something went wrong. The first 5 or 6 are easy to come up with but keep plugging.

Below is my 10-minute list of things that went horribly wrong in my business life.

1. When I worked in circulation at Victoria Secret Catalogue, I had a $200,000 error in my Excel spreadsheet.

2. When I was fired at Victoria's Secret Catalogue, and it wasn't because of the $200,000 error.

3. The Japanese project at VSC — Victoria Secret Catalogue Goes to Japan and Murphy's Law Truly Exists.

4. When I shouted out "shut up" at a company party watching the MTV world premiere of Michael Jackson Thriller music video.

5. When I was a banker for Barnett Bank in Ft. Myers, FL, Fowler street branch, and I got conned.

6. While managing Ken's Pizza in Griffin, GA, I noticed my yield was declining in my beer sales and how I discovered the culprit.

7. What happened when I left my computer/AV adapter for my MacBook Air in my hotel room 10 miles away.

8. That time my flight was diverted from DC to Baltimore because of weather, and people were losing their minds.

9. The experience of teaching the chapter on issuing bonds in my first accounting class at the college level.

10. When I got a promotion at Price Waterhouse and discovered my percentage pay increase was not proportional to others promoted to the same position.

Mining

Pick one of the items on your list and start mining the facts surrounding your story. What are the details surrounding the story, knowing no detail is too small? In doing this, think, "what facts does the audience need to know?" This can include, "who is the story about?" Who else is part of the story and their relationship to you?

What is the setting? What is the hero's goal, and is this something that you wanted to accomplish but it got derailed (conflict)?

By way of example, let's take #9 from my list: Teaching the chapter on issuing bonds in my first accounting class at the college level. My details/facts during the mining phase include:

- Franklin University
- Adjunct faculty
- My very first accounting course I taught
- Marsha Adams
- Late in the fall term
- The word amortization, which they got hung up on
- I described something wrong early in the lecture and it went south after that
- Confused about the relationship of the interest rates when the bond was being underwritten and when it was sold
- 20 students in the class with 5 accounting majors

Now that you have listed these facts, go back and think of things that could raise the stakes even if you are embellishing the story a bit, so you can create more tension and keep the audience's attention. For example, the more I tried to explain the concept of what a bond premium was using the interest difference, the more confused and frustrated the class became ... which got my anger up to a point that half of the class began to cry and the other half wanted to punch me out. This did not actually happen, but it sure felt like it at the time, and a joke about it now helps convey the intensity of the moment. Just pushing the envelope, a bit, raising the stakes (a tad of appropriate embellishment is needed). The reason for this? The more important the situation is, the more impactful are the stumbling blocks that create emotion and it is the *emotion* that helps us to remember the story and the resolution.

Think about business storytelling this way — you are not giving a deposition, you are trying to get your message across to the audience. Also, a story is not a chronological order of facts. It is the backdrop or launchpad for your message, linked to your goal or aim for what you want your audience to *do* as a result of listening to your presentation, and it's all wrapped up with emotion.

The more important the situation is, the more impactful are the stumbling blocks that create emotion and it is the *emotion* that helps us to remember the story and the resolution.

If you take the time to think about those times in your life when things went wrong, and then select one anecdote and go mining, you will be amazed at the number of stories you have. In discovering those stories, you'll suddenly be well on your way to taking the numb out of the numbers. Some people think you are just telling a story to tell a story. On the contrary! Stories are used to clarify or enlighten a challenging idea.

Takeaways

- The first step is to identify. Identify things that you are trying to solve, challenges that you are facing, or things that started off well but then went sideways. And begin a list.

- Mining comes next. Choose one item from your list and begin mining all the details surrounding that issue.

- You are not giving a deposition; you are trying to get your message across to the audience.

Chapter 8

CRAFTING THE STORY

> *"A chef is a mixture maybe of artistry and craft. You have to learn the craft really to get there."*
>
> — Wolfgang Puck

Now that you have a lot of facts and details, let's move in the P.R.O.V. portion of the I.M.P.R.O.V. story system.

Pivot

This is where everything is going well and then something changes (pivot, the surprise) and now the conflict has been introduced and the tension begins to rise. This is your transition from the beginning to the middle of the story.

By adding a little embellishment to my mining piece in the previous chapter, I have moved right into the part when everything begins to go wrong and gets out of control. (Fear not! Out-of-control story topics put you *in* control of your audience once you know how to use stories to achieve your aims.)

Raise

This is where we raise the stakes and increase the tension in the story. Think about the things that went wrong or could have gone wrong after the pivot. Take a moment and list 3-7 things that did go wrong or could have gone wrong after that moment. This is where you add more conflict and make the tension increase as you tell the story. This keeps the audience's attention on you and not their smartphones.

Raising the stakes in the story about me explaining bond amortization to my first class of college students, I came up with the following details, embellishments, and exaggerations to help make my point.

It got so tense in the classroom everyone needed a break, but I was not going to give them a break until they understood the concept.

One student stood up and gave me the finger and walked out of class.

The classroom got so loud that three other business professors came in to see what is going on. I asked them to take a seat and tried to explain bonds to them. They got more confused than the students and tried to untangle the students and ignored me.

A student who was sitting in the back of class was recording this whole incident on his cell phone and posted parts on his Facebook, Twitter and Instagram accounts and hashtagged me #AccountingProfessorIdiot. This turned into a social media nightmare.

Now we will begin to transition the middle to the end of the story.

Out

It's time to wrap the story up. There are a couple ways to end the story and we are not looking for a "they lived happily ever after" moment. We are looking to make our point in telling this story. You can step out of the story and relate it to their world. For example:

- In retrospect, I learned _____.

- Thinking about this differently, I would
  have done _____.

- What I learned was _____.

- Knowing what I know now,
  I would have _____.

How many of you have been in this situation before?

In the bond case, just as I am transitioning from the middle to the end of the story, I would step out and say, "How many of you have been in this situation before ... where you are trying to explain what seems like to be a simple concept, and totally confuse your audience? This is an example of the curse of knowledge." Then I would move into the solution that I came up with to solve the students' problem.

Another approach involves realizing that you don't have to end the story. You can step out of the story and relate it to their world. For example, "How many of you have been faced with this?" Then continue with, "What I have learned from this is ..." Here is your opportunity to offer the big/key lesson or your call to action.

Victory

Congratulate yourself for developing your story and making it relatable to the message, issue, or challenge you are experiencing.

At this point, you have everything you need to write your story. Below is my story about the teaching of bonds in an introduction to financial accounting course.

I was three-quarters of the way through my first academic semester teaching at the college level and was feeling good about myself. My course was Introduction to Financial Accounting and my students appeared to enjoy my teaching style. I was able to use my humor and practical examples to help make a dry subject more interesting.

Then came the lecture on issuing bonds and how to account for them. It started out well when I was describing that a bond is issued to raise money — like borrowing money from the bank or using a credit card. Then everything went south when I was trying to explain that when the bond is underwritten, it is assigned an interest rate which is the amount of return the company will pay those who purchase the bonds. A number of students cocked their heads in confusion. You know the look — the furrowed brows, the skeptical grimaces, the tilted heads.

Then I explained that when the bond is sold to the public that the prevailing market interest rate will determine if the buyers are willing to pay more or less for the bond. Everyone still look confused — they were staring at me but had stopped taking notes. Did I stop and ask why they looked confused? Of course not; I just kept plugging head.

Then I said that if the bond was underwritten at an interest rate greater than the current market rate, people would want to pay less for the bond and the difference would be called a premium. Now eyes began to cross and glaze over.

At that point, I realized that I was wrong and tried to correct the issue. I apologized and said, "I am sorry but I am wrong." (I had meant to say MORE! They are willing to pay more, not less.)

Oh my god, it was a simple slip of the tongue but I had lost them. They were tired and confused and blood-in-the-water sharky in their willingness to attack me for my mistake. A student asked, "So, wait. That's wrong? I don't follow. What's wrong? The rate or the premium? Or what they are willing to pay?" I felt my hands start to sweat as I overheard another student say to the girl behind her: "It's his first class. I overheard him say that to another faculty member, just before he walked in. It's going to be a long semester." I could practically hear their eyes rolling and feel my credibility crumbling. I felt like a high school substitute teacher — ripe for ridicule on the students' home turf, where I was a stranger and an amateur.

I was feeling like I was being attacked and shouted, "I MADE A MISTAKE. IF YOU WILL JUST GIVE ME A CHANCE TO EXPLAIN, I WILL FIX THIS." I just made things even worse. I had just yelled at my college students over a mistake that I had made. I said, "What I MEANT TO SAY WAS if the bond was underwritten at an interest rate that is greater than the current market rate, people would want to pay more for the bond and the difference would be called a premium." One of the students interjected, "That's what you said the first time; you just repeated yourself." To which I replied, "No I didn't, the first time I said, 'if the bond was underwritten at an interest rate that is greater than the current market rate, people would want to pay less for the bond and the difference would be called a premium and I just corrected myself and said if the bond was underwritten at an interest rate that is greater than the current market rate, people would want to pay more for the bond and the difference would be called a premium." The whole class let out a sigh of exasperation. They weren't understanding and they weren't amused by me in the least.

One student was so frustrated he stood up, gave me the finger as a half-hearted parting gestured, and walked out of class. One student put his head on his desk in defeat. I felt like I was going to cry. Factions began to form among the students and I was losing the class. They were trying to explain the concept to each other, and some where just talking about me and how ridiculous this was. I took a deep breath and replied, "I DIDN'T SIMPLY REPEAT MYSELF. I just misspoke and said 'less' when I meant to say 'more.' Why don't you guys understand what I am trying to say? It's not that hard." And then I'd really done it. I'd insulted their intelligence, after confusing them and then yelling at them. Truly, not a shining moment in my teaching career.

Has this ever happened to you? *The more you try to explain a complex accounting topic to those who don't have the same depth and breadth of your knowledge, the more you end up confusing people and possibly losing your temper? What I should have done differently was to spend more time in preparing for the class and putting myself back in their shoes and remembering how confused I once was, too, when trying to understand this concept. I should have tried to use simpler language and put it in a context that they could relate to. I should have used numbers to explain the difference in the interest rates. And I should have paid attention to their body language, slowed down, and controlled my temper. Bottomline, I was not prepared well enough and learned a very valuable and painful lesson that day.*

To become a better business storyteller starts with stories that are personal because they help you to connect with your audience on a human level. These personal stories can be incorporated into your business storytelling because they are very relatable to your audience. While the story above had elements of dread, embarrassment, and humor, business stories can use any type of emotion or style; they can make us laugh or cry or sit up with a big "ah ha." Once you get comfortable in developing your stories, then developing stories that help *take the numb out of the numbers* becomes second nature.

Once you get comfortable in developing your stories, then developing stories that help *take the numb out of the numbers* becomes second nature.

Takeaways

- Remember to Pivot in your story and introduce the conflict.
- Raise the stakes by creating more tension in the story.
- Get OUT of the story by sharing your message or lesson that you have learned.

Chapter 9

STORYTELLING IN BUSINESS IS A GREAT STRATEGY

"Every business has a story to tell."

— Jay Baer

Storytelling in business can be a rather misunderstood process. If you think business storytelling is like telling fairytales, think again. I'm not talking about stories like Jack and the Beanstalk, Little Red Riding Hood, or Sleeping Beauty. Every day we are exposed to storytelling from major companies and their brands through television commercials, print and social media ads, and various online messages. Even product packaging tells a story. If you've ever watched a Super Bowl, you have participated in one of the best examples of this kind of storytelling. Those commercials are designed to tell stories that connect on an emotional level with the viewer to drive buying habits. Telling stories in business is big business.

Telling stories in business is big business.

Do you remember the ad that ultimately changed the way Super Bowl commercials were designed and developed? It was Apple's 1984 commercial introducing the Macintosh computer, and it revolutionized the way companies advertised. It was so innovative that *Advertising Age*, the "bible" for advertising agencies, named this commercial number one on its list of the greatest 50 commercials of all time. Without using a competitor's name or even showing the new Macintosh, Apple told their story: IBM dominated the market, controlled its customers, and Apple was going to give them a run for their money. They tied it all back to George Orwell's book *1984* and created a visual message that was disturbing and memorable. At his keynote address to Apple in 1983, Steve Jobs told the same story. IBM wanted it all and had aimed its guns on the last obstacle to industry control: Apple. Will Big Blue (IBM) dominate the entire computer industry? The whole information age? Was Orwell right about 1984?

Take a journey through YouTube and search for the top Super Bowl commercials of all time. Each one of them has some emotional effect on the audience. A few of my favorites are Pepsi's commercial featuring Cindy Crawford, the Coke ad featuring Mean Joe Greene, the McDonald's commercial featuring the showdown between Larry Bird and Michael Jordan, and the annual adorable Budweiser puppy.

Puppies, heroes, and humor create a strong emotional response in our brains. Research shows that during tense moments in a story, our brain produces a stress hormone called cortisol, which allows us to focus. During cute moments of a story, our brain releases oxytocin, the chemical that elevates our connection and empathy (also known as the "cuddle hormone"). During happy moments, our brains release dopamine, which makes us feel optimistic.

Storytelling — and the chemicals it helps to release in our brains — also helps consumers to open our wallets and buy products from companies or give to charities. Storytelling prompts us to change attitudes and beliefs, to empathize with others, and to learn more effectively because stories increase retention and understanding. Storytelling is powerful, it is strategic, and it has measurable, meaningful results.

The next time you prepare to engage with an audience (and the size of that audience can be from one person to 1,000 people), craft your information into a compelling story. You will increase your success — whether success is measured as a donation to a not-for-profit, a product sold, or prospective client won over.

Takeaways

- Advertisements like commercials are designed to tell stories that connect on an emotional level with the viewer to drive buying habits.

- Telling stories creates a strong emotional response in our brains.

- Storytelling (and the chemicals that are released in our brains) also motivates us to buy or give, change our attitudes and beliefs, empathize with others, and learn more effectively.

Chapter 10

THE DARK SIDE OF STORYTELLING

"You don't want another Enron? Here's your law: If a company can't explain, in one sentence, what it does ... it's illegal."

— Lewis Black

Storytelling, when used for good, will help grow your business, your reputation, and your brand. However, when storytelling is used to deceive or to commit fraud, it will ultimately crush your business, your reputation, and your brand. That crush may also come with the potential of spending time where orange is the new black (i.e., prison).

Think about some of the greatest fraudsters of all time — Barry Minkow, Bernie Madoff, and Dennis Kozlowski. The one thing they had in common: They all told a compelling story. But when you pulled back the curtain, you found a complex house of cards that could not stand up to scrutiny. There are many instances where corporate storytelling did significant damage to companies and their brands. Three of my favorite examples are Enron, Theranos, and JC Penney.

In the book, *What's Your Story?: Storytelling to Move Markets, Audiences, People, and Brands,* the authors discuss the "Ken Lay Story."[10] Ken Lay was the son of a poor Baptist preacher in the small town of Tyrone, Missouri. Through hard work and dedication, he became a Naval officer, earned his doctorate in economics, was the chief economist at Exxon, was a federal energy regulator, and then became undersecretary for the Department of the Interior. His successes led him to be the founder and CEO of Enron Corporation.

Ken Lay's story is a classic story. A poor person living in small-town USA, fighting against all the odds to become one of the most powerful and wealthiest men in the energy industry, whose company at its peak had an estimated market value of $70 billion. That was before its collapse. In this story, the early hero is Ken Lay, and the villains are the number of obstacles he had to overcome in his rise to power. However, when Mr. Lay's moral ethics shifted, his company failed, and he went on to become a convicted felon. The hero became the villain.

In a *Harvard Business Review* case study, "A Tale of Storytelling: Its Allure and Its Traps," Hilary Austen argues that it is the departure from the truth that makes the story the winner.[11] Actual experiences are rooted in complexities that our minds have a hard time grasping — data, stats, figures. "When we tell a story, we are not giving a deposition" is a phrase I have heard a lot from storytellers in the National Speakers Association (NSA). We are "departing from the truth," as Austen says, or taking creative license as we embellish,

---

10   Mathews, Ryan D., and Wacker, Watts, What's Your Story? Storytelling to Move Markets, Audiences, People, and Brands, FT Press, 1st edition (August 30, 2007).

11   Austen, Hilary. "A Tale of Storytelling: Its Allure and Its Traps," Harvard Business Review, Case Study, 2014, https://hbr.org/product/a-tale-of-storyt elling-its-allure-and-its-traps/ROT235-PDF-ENG.

create tension, and paint a picture to enhance the story. This effort at divergence can, however, go too far, as is reflected in the story that Enron was using when their business model changed from pipes-in-the-ground oil drilling to natural gas and commodities. This story was so incredibly compelling that *Fortune* magazine named Enron "America's Most Innovative Company" for six years in a row. Enron moved their business model from tangible assets to intangible ones and telling the story of how innovative they were. Behind the scenes, what Enron was doing was applying a loose accounting definition to mark to market accounting whereby booking current revenue on hypothetical future assumptions that could not be substantiated. Innovative maybe, but not the truth. (If you want to learn more about the details around Enron, read the book *The Smartest Guys in the Room* by Bethany McLean and Peter Elkind or watch the documentary "The Smartest Guys in the Room" by Magnolia Pictures.)

What's Your Story? discusses the difference between "truth" and "true." They use an example of Procter & Gamble and their detergent, Tide. A P&G research scientist sitting in the lab used expensive equipment to prove that Tide cleans laundry better than the competition. That is the true statement. However, laundry rooms throughout the United States do not come staffed with scientists or expensive equipment; those who purchase laundry detergents decide about which brand to purchase based on what they believe is the truth. In most cases, the truth is derived from an advertisement that might state "my clothes are cleaner when I used Tide versus other brands." In other words, corporate storytelling is about *truth statements* ("my clothes are brighter and whiter since I switched!") rather than *true statements* ("scientists in a lab have data that shows that clothing washed in Tide has fewer dirt particles after washing than similarly soiled clothing washed with a different brand of detergent").

Another *What's Your Story?* case study highlights what happened to JC Penney from 2011 to 2013. In 2011, JC Penney hired Ron Johnson, the former senior vice president of retail operations at Apple Inc., to be their next CEO. Ron's story was one of transformation, bringing the brand back to its original stature as a leading department store. He was going to fix JC Penney's complex pricing structure (including doing away with coupons and sales), attract both the Millennial generation and a more affluent customer base, and create new, exciting shopping experiences. His "truth story" was so compelling that it convinced company stakeholders, many on Wall Street and celebrities like Ellen DeGeneres and Martha Stewart, to invest heavily or add their names and product lines to the transformation.

Unfortunately, Johnson forgot to take into consideration his existing customer base — which was, in fact, almost the exact opposite of the customer demographic that would respond to the new-and-improved JC Penney. He was telling the stakeholders what they wanted to hear, but forgot to include one true statement about the current customer base: They were middle-of-the-road bargain shoppers. Because of the unrealistic expectations, he was not only unable to attract the young and the rich as customers, he also alienated the true JC Penney's customer. In 2013, sales dropped 28%, the company's revenues declined by $1 billion and the stock price was half of what it was before Ron's vison. No surprise, Ron was fired.

Now consider another example of storytelling gone bad, this time from the medical device industry. The *Harvard Business Review* article titled "Theranos and the Dark Side of Storytelling" discusses Elizabeth Holmes, the founder of the blood testing company

Theranos.[12] The company claimed to possess the technology to test a wide variety of diseases from a small amount of blood drawn from a pricked finger. Elizabeth Holmes's story is compelling because she was an extremely bright 19-year-old student at Stanford University who dropped out of school to found Theranos. According to the article, her vision was to save millions of lives around the world through her technology.

Her story and her mission were so compelling that in 2015 her company was valued at $9 billion and *Forbes* magazine named her the youngest self-made female billionaire in the world. Her storytelling was so convincing that she recruited well-known political types, such as Henry Kissinger, George Schultz, Sam Nunn, and Col. James Mattis, to be on her Board of Directors.

In October 2015, the *Wall Street Journal* reported that the company's blood testing technology was a near-total failure.[13] According to an exposé in *Vanity Fair*, the Elizabeth Holmes story was told and retold so many times that it became more the story of innovation and female empowerment than the story of Ms. Holmes.[14] The company was founded on the story and, based on current evidence, the story is fictional at best.

---

12 Gottschall, Jonathan, "Theranos and the Dark Side of Storytelling," *Harvard Business Review*, Oct. 18, 2016, https://hbr.org/2016/10/theranos-and-the-dark-side-of-storytelling.

13 Carreyrou, John, "Hot Startup Theranos Has Struggled With Its Blood-Test Technology," *Wall Street Journal*, October 2015, https://www.wsj.com/articles/theranos-has-struggled-with-blood-tests-1444881901.

14 Bilton, Nick, "Exclusive: How Elizabeth Holmes's House of Cards Came Tumbling Down," *Vanity Fair*, September 2016, https://www.vanityfair.com/news/2016/09/elizabeth-holmes-theranos-exclusive.

The Elizabeth Holmes story was told and retold so many times that it became more the story of innovation and female empowerment than the story of Ms. Holmes.

Storytelling can, indeed, span the spectrum of the proverbial good, the bad, and the ugly. Ugly storytelling examples, like the Enron and Theranos situations, are deliberately concocted to deceive and defraud an organization and its investors. JC Penney's situation, however, is different because there was no ill-intent. It's bad but it's not ugly. It was the new CEO's vision on how to transform the business that blinded people. The fault lies with the JC Penney Board of Directors who were collectively enamored by the new story. They didn't analyze the story they loved against the facts they knew to be true to determine how this new vision of the company would affect their business and customer base. As for the good stories — the ones intended to help stakeholders learn, be inspired, trust you, and move to action — those are the stories I hope to help you write. So whether you're seeking to *take the numb out of numbers* or the boredom out of any business topic, your new-found storytelling skills should be a great boon to your success.

This chapter about the dark side of storytelling is an important one to include in this book because it's vital that you understand that not all stories are created equally, and that telling a great story — if told under false pretenses or if disconnected from data and realities — is not enough to ensure your wild success. It's important that we recognize the stories behind actions, and how their compelling nature draws us to them. In other words, the stories must be congruent with the actualities of the business, supported by the financial statements. We must ask questions and determine the real character of those actions and whether they stand up as the truth. Even the story Ken Lay finely crafted for Enron had cracks that should have revealed the fraud. In fact, there was one investor who didn't invest a dime into Enron and was even chastised in financial periodicals and by pundits for his decision. That investor was Warren Buffett. The reason he did not invest into Enron was that he could not make sense of Enron's business model and how it related to the company financial statements. His logic superseded his emotions in his decision-making process. Reason prevailed, and Buffett came out ahead.

In the end, we all love a good story, especially when told by a gifted storyteller. They draw us in, inspire us, and motivate us to action. I simply encourage you to remember that not all stories are positive or innocuous, and that the onus is on us — as recipients of stories we hear or read — to validate the stories that seem thin, to checks the facts when necessary, and to trust our guts when it comes to the stories that drive our behaviors and belief

---

Storytelling, despite it being a positive and powerful tool in most circumstances, it will ultimately crush your business, your reputation, and your brand if you use it to deceive or to commit fraud.

Takeaways

- Storytelling, despite it being a positive and powerful tool in most circumstances, it will ultimately crush your business, your reputation, and your brand if you use it to deceive or to commit fraud.

- Corporate storytelling is about *truth* statements rather than *true* statements.

- The story and the facts must be congruent; if not, then you must investigate.

Section 2

BE AMAZING AND ENGAGING

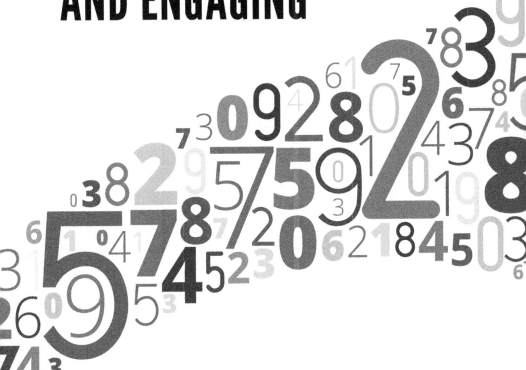

Chapter 11

STEP #1 OF BEING AMAZING AND ENGAGING – GETTING PAST YOUR FEAR

> *"There are two types of speakers: Those who get nervous and those who are liars."*
>
> — Mark Twain

Getting Past Your Fear of Public Speaking

Your heart is racing, your palms are sweaty, your mouth is dry as the Mojave Desert. You don't have butterflies — you have a Cinereous Vulture flying in your stomach! You feel nauseated and want to run away, but you can't because 100 people are waiting to hear your presentation. You are experiencing glossophobia: the fear of public speaking.

According to teachthought.com, "5 Quotes to Help Overcome the Fear of Public Speaking," 80 million Americans are afraid to speak in front of large groups of people.[15] 80 million people represents a population about 10 times the number of people who live in New York City. The fear of public speaking beat out the fear of drowning, needles, snakes, heights, and even clowns (eek!).

Overcoming your fear of speaking in front of a group is difficult. Sometimes even the thought of overcoming your fear of speaking can be crippling! So what can you do?

6 Tips for Getting Past Your Fear

First, realize you are not alone! Even professional speakers like me get a little nervous before a presentation. Working with clients, I help everyone understand that standing in front a group and presenting is an acquired skill. Here are six teaser tips to help you to get past your fear, with even more information in the next three chapters.

Tip #1: Be Prepared

Be the expert and know your subject. There is a difference between preparation and perfection, and no presentation is perfect. Yes, you will make a mistake, maybe more than one. Most of the time, unless it's a real blooper, the only person who will know about it is you.

There is a difference between preparation and perfection, and no presentation is perfect.

---

15   TeachThought, "5 Quotes to Help Overcome the Fear of Public Speaking," August 29, 2017, https://www.teachthought.com/technology/5-quotes-to-help-overcome-the-fear-of-public-speaking/.

Being prepared goes beyond being the expert. Preparation is knowledge of the subject and the ability to express the information in plain English, so you can engage your audience in a conversation versus a lecture. Throughout this book, you'll continue to learn different strategies and techniques to help translate your technical knowledge into information that will inspire action.

Tip #2: Silence Your Inner Critic

It's hard to ignore that voice in your head that constantly gives you negative feedback about your presentation. "You don't like speaking in front of crowds" or "You are terrible at this, you should have called in sick." On especially bad days, it says "Your audience will not like you, and you will come off looking stupid."

Silence that voice by using the improv technique of "Yes, and ..." to boost your confidence. Try saying out loud "Yes! And, I'm prepared because I am the expert on this topic." Or "Yes! And, I may not like speaking in front of crowds, but I am prepared, and I accept that I am nervous." Or maybe "Yes! And, I am not terrible at this. I just haven't had many opportunities to present, so I am a little rusty." Remember, the story that you tell yourself will dictate the outcome.

An Assistant Professor of psychology at Kellogg School of Management at Northwestern University, Amy Cuddy was terrified about giving a presentation. However, her TED talk "Your Body Language Shapes Who You Are" remains one of the top 10 most viewed TED Talks.[16] She overcame her fear by telling herself that she is confident in her presentation skills, even though she wasn't.

---

16   Cuddy, Amy, "Your Body Language Shapes Who You Are," TEDGlobal 2012, June 2012, https://www.ted.com/talks/amy_cuddy_your_body_language_shapes_who_you_are?referrer=playlist-the_most_popular_talks_of_all.

This positive self-talk increased her chances of success. On stage during her TED Talk, she says, "Don't fake it till you make it. Fake it till you become it." In other words, preparation, silencing your inner critic, and finding the opportunities will lead to greater confidence and success.

Tip #3: Practice

How do you get to Carnegie Hall? Practice, practice, practice! Okay, old comedian material aside, you must practice your presentation. Practicing before your presentation is a must! There are two pieces of advice that never work, and they are: Picture the audience naked and practice in front of a mirror.

There are two pieces of advice that never work, and they are: Picture the audience naked and practice in front of a mirror.

First, seeing the audience naked would make me more nervous, very uncomfortable, and possibly nauseated. Second, when you are practicing in front of a mirror, you are just looking at your reflection. Is that who you are speaking to? No.

The best advice that a National Speaker Association member gave me was to practice where you will deliver your presentation, or at least a similar room or space. Use a camera to video yourself, so you can watch it and make necessary adjustments. Bring family and friends to watch you practice to offer honest, constructive feedback. Also, and this is very important, know your opening (and closing) comments well. How you begin your presentation can dictate the overall success you will have. A strong opening will help calm your nerves and increase your confidence, and a strong closing will end your presentation on a confident note.

These positive practice techniques will lead to greater success.

Tip #4: It's ALL About Your Audience

Any time you present to a group, you should provide useful solutions for them. You want them to walk away with tips and tools to make their life easier, solve a problem, or expand their skills. Don't focus on how you look to the audience. Switch that thought to how your presentation will help them. My new mantra is "It starts with me, AND it is not about me, it's about them." Focus on them, your audience, and deliver the benefits that they want.

Tip #5: You Can Control Your Nerves

Before I speak I always have a case of the butterflies, and that is okay. I want to be a little nervous because that helps keep me on my toes and ready for the presentation. I did not, however, develop that strategy overnight. To be honest, when I was first starting out, I was very nervous. I practiced specific techniques to calm my nerves, things I do to this day.

Deep-breathing exercises in the morning of and right before a presentation help get more oxygen to the brain and slow down your wildly spinning inner clock. Drink plenty of water to stay hydrated. Our brains need to be properly hydrated to operate at peak performance. Too much caffeine will do the opposite and increase your level of nervousness.

Arrive at least 45 minutes early to make sure everything is set up, and your equipment is operating properly. When everything is working, it's time for you to work the room. Greet the attendees and thank them for coming to your presentation. By doing this, you remove the barrier between you and the audience, which helps reduce your level of nervousness. Become a student of public speaking and seek out other opportunities to present in front of an audience, no matter the size. The more comfortable you are in front of an audience, the less nervous you will be.

Tip #6: Be Authentic

Watch and take note of what dynamic speakers do. When I watch other speakers, I pick up on nuances of their presentation style, not to copy them but to help me become the best I can be. When I am presenting, I am myself (not Tony Robbins, Bill Clinton, or Steve Jobs), but that doesn't mean I haven't learned from watching them speak. I am authentic to me and my style, and what helps in being authentic is being passionate about your topic. When you are passionate, it comes through in your voice and your body language. You are not as nervous because you are talking about something you believe in and care about. You are not lecturing; you are having a conversation. When you do this, the fear goes away. When you lack passion, your fear factor is high because you are not living Tip #1. (That is called a callback in comedy.)

Take these six tips and put them to use. They are the foundation to get past your fear so you can deliver a compelling and engaging presentation.

Takeaways

- Always be thoroughly prepared.
- Put some duct tape over the mouth of your inner critic.

- Be you! Don't try to be Tony Robbins. There is only one Tony Robbins, so go out and be the best YOU.

Dealing with the Peanut Gallery That Is Your Inner Critic

> *"Your inner critic is simply a part of you that needs more self-love."*
>
> — Amy Leigh Mercree

Whether you are in front of an audience or sharing thoughts during a meeting, and you see all those eyeballs leveled at you, employing the principles of improvisation will save you. The greatest improv principle for overcoming this fear? Silencing your inner critic.

The Reliable Inner Critic

That inner critic of yours never goes on vacation — it's there constantly giving opinions on anything and everything you do. In the case of speaking, the closer you get to the time you have to speak, the louder and more incessant the critic becomes. For a lot of people, they can get sick from the stress that the critic brings their way.

That inner critic of yours never goes on vacation – it's there constantly giving opinions on anything and everything you do.

What can you do? Well, first you must change the conversation in your head and start programming your brain to use "yes, and ..." instead of "yes, but ...." What do I mean by this? Think about the difference between "but" vs. "and." Using "but" introduces a contrasting thought and stops the other in its tracks. "And" connects one thought with other — allowing both to be considered jointly. For instance, you could be saying to yourself, "Yes, you have been asked to give this presentation, but you'll do awful." Or, you could turn it into the following, "Yes, you have been asked to give this presentation, and you can do it." When you make this switch, you develop confidence.

Consider the classic children's story by Watty Piper, *The Little Engine That Could*, which teaches this very principle.[17] Each of the different locomotives in the story could be considered inner critics — each pointing out a reason the little engine couldn't accomplish the task at hand. Eventually, the little engine, which had been told she wasn't fast enough, big enough, or powerful enough, was the best locomotive for an important job. Despite the doubts and criticism, the train, as we all know, chanted repeatedly to herself, "I think I can, I think I can, I think I can." And she did.

"You're not fast enough," "You're not smart enough," "You're not interesting enough." Your inner critic needs to be reprimanded and corrected. And guess what? You have the power to do it. Tell yourself, "I can do this," and the more times you repeat it, the more you will believe it. This positive programming of the brain is real and can be used to overcome your immediate fears. The more you say it, the more you will silence that droning voice of doom that cycles through all your fears: "You can't do this, you don't know what you're talking about, you're a fraud, you're going to fail, something will go wrong ..."

---

17   Piper, Watty, *The Little Engine That Could*, Philomel Books (September 27, 2005).

The Perfect Inner Critic

That last part of the inner critic's diatribe, "something will go wrong ...," is actually very likely to come true. If you expect perfection, you are likely to be disappointed. Yes, you will make a mistake, probably more than one, and just keep moving forward and don't mention the mistake. Your listeners won't pick up on it.

When you're overly focused on perfection, you can go into a downhill spiral if you do make some minor mistake, such as forgetting to make one of your less important points. If you maintain your confidence, something like that won't trip you up. You need to accept the fact that you will make some slips. Think of them as opportunities to learn to do even better.

Also, keep in mind, a certain amount of vulnerability goes a long way in winning over your audience. An excellent example of this is a TED Talk given by Megan Washington, an Australian singer/song-writer.[18] When she opens her speech, you are immediately aware that she has a speech impediment, or stutter. She goes on to say that, while she has no qualms about singing in front of people, she dreads public speaking. Throughout the presentation, the audience watches her struggle from time to time to get certain words out, but it doesn't matter. Her vulnerability has connected the audience to her, keeping them engaged. Then she shares a personal fact that you can't stutter when you sing. She then plays and sings a beautiful song perfectly, ending with a standing ovation from the crowd.

---

18 Washington, Megan, "Why I Live in Mortal Dread of Public Speaking," TEDxSydney 2014, April 2014, https://www.ted.com/talks/ megan_washington_why_i_live_in_mortal_dread_of_public_speaking#t-19134.

While we may not have the opportunity to leverage a vulnerability like this, it's important to remember: the inner critic will tell you far more than you need to know. You will hear what you simply cannot do or how you will screw up. And here is what you can tell that naysayer: "Yes, I know I will make mistakes, and they will not hamper me. Yes, I will not be perfect, and that means I can only get better." Even today, whenever I get up in front of people, I get butterflies, but I can control them now and make them flutter in the direction of my choice.

Reasoning with the Inner Critic

With all this bad-mouthing of the inner critic, it's only fair that I admit that it does serve a purpose. If I were to consider delivering a speech on nuclear physics, I would hope that my inner critic would start screaming at me long before I stood at the lectern. The critic doesn't know when to shut up, however, and that's where you need to train it. You might know enough about a topic to deliver a decent speech, but the critic keeps nagging: "Your nose hair is showing. Your tie is crooked. What a nitwit." If you pay too much attention, the prophecies of failure could come true. You get hung up on your shortcomings rather than focusing on your strengths.

Sometimes the key is to just confront it: "Shut up! Shut up!" You can accomplish this through the "yes, and ..." approach of improv. "Yes, I hear what you're saying, And I'm going to do it anyway." The critic may still try to undermine you but not as loudly. You'll build up self-esteem. You'll feel confident. You'll go and do it.

Takeaways

- Use "Yes! And ..." in dealing with the reliable inner critic.

- Know that you will make a mistake and, most of the time, you are the only one who knows.

- Pay attention to what the reliable critic is saying and only take on projects that you are the expert.

Controlling Feelings of Anxiety

"People become attached to their burdens sometimes more than the burdens are attached to them."

— George Bernard Shaw

I've been constantly reminded of the need to understand my limits. As a diabetic, for example, I must listen to what my body is telling me all the time. If my blood sugar is calling for me to tweak my schedule, I must listen and adapt. When you are aware of the signals, no matter your specific situation, you will know what to do — and that's true whether you're trying to pick up on the messages that your body is sending you or on the messages that an audience is sending you. It is the awareness itself that plays a major role in reducing stress.

Improvisation and awareness have helped me manage stress so that I can take better care of myself — allowing me to better respond and plan my next step. The skills of improvisation clearly are a strength in times of crisis. As you listen, assess, and adapt to each scenario presented to you, you can more effectively overcome anything. And as you do it more and more, you become confident that you are indeed able to deal with a situation. As a result, your confidence increases ... while your stress decreases.

If you understand that you can control how your body reacts to a medical condition, then you should also be able to understand that you can control feelings of anxiety when confronted with a new and uncomfortable situation. We all have found ourselves facing appearances we might prefer to avoid, whether we're called into the office or hauled into court or going on a job interview or delivering a speech. Again, you have the power to silence that inner critic's prognostications of impending failure. Tell yourself, "Yes, this feels difficult for me, and I can do it."

There is a huge difference between "I will do the best I can" and "This is going to fail."

We must do a lot of things that we don't want to tackle. Those tasks become much harder if we cop a bad attitude. "I hate talking to people and networking" will defeat any chance of doing well at such activities. There is a huge difference between "I will do the best I can" and "This is going to fail." If you adopt a better attitude, one that doesn't broadcast defeat, you might find that you are doing pretty well. You can feel good about your accomplishment.

Whether your stress results from a physical condition or something else, so much depends on your ability to perceive things positively. Either you win, or you let the stress win. Your choice.

Takeaways

- Listen and adapt to what your body is telling you.
- Put more duct tape over the inner critic's mouth.
- Keep a positive mental attitude and don't let the stress win.

Dealing with the Unknowns of Public Speaking

> *"Feel the fear of public speaking and do it anyway."*
>
> — Arvee Robinson

As stated earlier, public speaking is one of greatest fears people can have. There are many reasons fueling this fear, but the unpredictable variables that come from speaking no doubt add to the anxiety. You probably know what I'm going to suggest combatting these fears — that's right, improvisation. I'm going to present a few common scenarios that can occur when needing to speak publicly and how improv can help you avoid a panicked meltdown at the podium.

When Heads Start Bobbing

I've seen people fall asleep within 15 minutes during an hour-long presentation. If you do enough speaking, you're going to see heads bobbing, particularly at all-day workshops and seminars. The unfortunate part of that is when people walk out of a presentation that is simply not engaging enough to hold their full attention, about a two-thirds of what they heard stays behind them in the room. They don't retain it. Within two weeks they barely remember anything — not even the name of the speaker. Think about the investment wasted (theirs *and* yours).

While it's very much the attendee's job to be respectful and stay awake, it is just as much your responsibility to engage your audience to make staying awake easier.

While it's very much the attendee's job to be respectful and stay awake, it is just as much your responsibility to engage your audience to make staying awake easier. You must do this through connecting with them, which isn't going to happen by rattling off a bunch of bullet points in a monotone voice. Think of your audience as a one-on-one interaction — try to create a relationship together. You can do this by giving examples to illustrate the material or introduce exercises that require participation.

Something to keep in mind: You're not going to connect with everyone. There will always be someone sitting there that clearly projects, "My boss made me come to this." You can't do much about that person. But as for the rest of them, you can focus on making that connection that will keep them engaged and focused on your message.

The Show Must Go On

There will be times where what was planned for simply gets thrown out the window. Maybe there's a technical malfunction preventing you from using your computer and slides, someone cancelled in a lineup of speakers and you need to unexpectedly change the time when you present, the fire alarm goes off and everyone needs to leave the building and you return an hour later, or your keynote has been cut from one hour to 30 minutes. The unpredictable is quite frankly predictable. Plan for things to not go as planned — or at least prepare yourself with the ability to be adaptable — yet another important element of improvisation.

I once heard a story about a gentleman who was giving a presentation and fell off the stage. He apparently misjudged a step. He tucked up and rolled, stood up, and continued his talk. He made it look as if he had done the stunt on purpose. Now that's what I call thorough preparation for any contingency! The lesson there is to take advantage of your forward momentum, whether you are stumbling literally or figuratively. On with the show.

Takeaways

- It is your responsibility to engage the audience and keep them awake.

- Be adaptable because something will always go wrong.

- Take advantage of your forward momentum, whether you are stumbling literally or figuratively. On with the show.

Chapter 12

STEP #2 OF BEING AMAZING AND ENGAGING – DEVELOPING YOUR PRESENTATION

> *"If you think presentations cannot enchant people, then you have never seen a really good one."*
>
> — Guy Kawaski

Developing Your Presentation from Scratch

Imagine this scenario. As a career-minded person, you are very open to ways you can advance your standing in your company. One day, your boss calls you into her office and informs you of a really great opportunity, one that could be a career-maker. You will be a speaker at a national industry conference, and your topic is "leadership challenges in today's disruptive business climate." Although you are well informed on the topic, you still need to build this presentation from the ground up. You go back to your office, stare at your computer, and realize you are not sure how to start building an outline, let alone a full presentation with a PowerPoint slide deck.

Most people would begin by creating an outline the way you were taught in grade school. The introduction will be Roman numeral one and the conclusion will be Roman numeral five. Other than that, you are unclear where to begin and what specific points to make. Of course, you could just type the title of your presentation into Google and see what pops up. Before searching the Internet, however, I suggest you use the clustering method to corral the knowledge you currently possess to develop the outline for your presentation.

Start by writing your topic in the middle of the page and circling it; in this case, write Leadership Challenges in the middle of the page. Then spend five minutes brainstorming everything you can think of that is associated with this topic. You may write down words and phrases like communication, social media, self-interests, attitude, culture, technology, complacency, managing change, broken processes, complacency, lack of new ideas. Write as many words as come to mind.

After you get all that knowledge out of your head and down on paper, group together words whose meanings are similar in nature. For example, self-interests, attitude, communication, and culture could be one grouping. Social media and technology could be another grouping; complacency, broken processes, and lack of new ideas could be another. Once you've identified your groupings, dig a bit deeper to determine what the words within each grouping have in common. Self-interests, attitude, communication, culture could have in common the corporate culture of the organization. The corporate culture of the organization now becomes a key point to the topic of your presentation. The words in each group are details to help build the content for this key point. Do the same exercise for each grouping. You now have the key points, or outline, for your presentation, and this is when you begin using online tools to build your presentation.

Once you've identified all your key points and the details of those key points, you can now transfer that information over to a Microsoft Word document. Start by using the software's outline feature to build your detailed outline for this presentation. As you input the information from your key points (groupings) into the Word document, other ideas and thoughts associated with the key point will arise. Be sure to capture that information as well. It's always better to have more content at this point — editing content out later is easier than going back to develop more ideas.

You might feel that this is obvious (you've used Word for decades) but don't skip ahead. I am going to share a tip that will save you time in building your PowerPoint slide deck, so stay with me.

From this outline, you can build your speech and your PowerPoint slide deck. Once your outline is built, close the file, and open a new PowerPoint presentation. Click *Insert* from the file menu, then choose the *down arrow* from the slides option, then select *slides from outline* option and then open the file containing your outline. Once this happens your outline is imported into your PowerPoint presentation. This is a new option in MS Office 365, and it is amazing. In full transparency, Chris Jenkins who is the CEO of the South Carolina Association of CPAs and an IT certified professional showed me this tip and it blew me away. This new tool blew me away so much that I totally abandoned the Apple Keynote software that I used for more than 10 years. Microsoft, you have a new advocate.

➤ Visit my YouTube Channel — The Accidental Accountant — to watch the tutorial I created.

Now you have the outline for your presentation in PowerPoint and a firm starting point to develop the supporting material. Once you have your speech and presentation nailed down, you can also create blog posts, articles, and social media postings from the same material. If you want to set yourself apart from other presenters, create a blog post, an article, and social media postings about your presentation. Send them in advance to the organization planning the conference so they can use it to help promote your session. That's what you call a meeting planner's dream come true.

If you want to set yourself apart from other presenters, create a blog post, an article, and social media postings about your presentation. Send them in advance to the organization planning the conference so they can use it to help promote your session.

Developing presentations using advanced online tools is what separates professionals from DIY presenters, and I want to give you insights into tools I have discovered and used. Later in this chapter, I will discuss developing an effective PowerPoint presentation. In addition, I will provide more timesaving tips about how you can bring content to life, including how to adjust fonts, how to work with templates, how to add something more unique than templates, and how to work with audio and video.

I have used the clustering method countless times to create presentations, articles, blog posts, and the roadmap for writing this book. It is a simple, easy way of getting your thoughts out of your head, so you can visualize and organize them, and so you can begin to develop a powerful, content driven presentation. Now go online and search "leadership challenges in today's disruptive business climate" and see what you can add to your presentation.

Takeaways

- Use the clustering method to get all the information on a specific topic out of your head and then on to paper.

- Organize your thoughts by grouping together words whose meanings are similar in nature.

- Use the PowerPoint tip to get started in developing your presentation.

Adding Visuals in Your Presentation

"Words are only postage stamps delivering the object for you to unwrap."

— George Bernard Shaw

Words can be very powerful, but not always as powerful as images. As we all know, "a picture is worth a thousand words!"

Microsoft PowerPoint is the most popular presentation software in today's business environment. There are other software products, such as Keynote and Prezi, but it appears that Microsoft has the corner on the market because, according to Microsoft, there are over 30 million PowerPoint presentations given worldwide every day. Who am I to argue with Microsoft?

Make A Visual Impact

Using visual aids in your presentation will create a greater impact and enhance the point you are trying to get across to your audience. Such visual aids can go well beyond PointPoint to include physical objects you hold up, show off, or even pass around the audience. At the TED2009 conference, Microsoft founder Bill Gates was delivering a presentation on malaria and how the disease was transmitted via mosquito bites. At one point in his presentation, Bill shouted at the audience, "Malaria is spread by mosquitoes and I brought some here in this jar." Then he released non-malaria infested mosquitos into the audience. Then he said, "Here, I'll let them roam around. There is no reason only poor people should be infected." Bill made his point to those who were in attendance, and the millions who have watched it since.

You can create a similar effect by using pictures, videos, sound bites, charts, and graphs in your presentation. John Media, the author of *Brain Rules*, states, "Vision trumps all other senses."[19] Our entire history has never been subjugated by books, email, or text messages. It was dominated by trees, cave drawings, and dinosaurs. Vision is important to us because most of the major threats to our lives are held visually. For example, while visiting Capri in Italy, my wife and

---

19   Medina, John, *Brain Rules: 12 Principles for Surviving and Thriving at Work, Home and School*, (Pear Press, Seattle, WA, 2014), 182.

I took a bus ride up to the top of the island. At one point, it appeared that the bus was about to go over the ledge and everyone on the bus gasped loudly and grabbed the railing in front of us to brace for the fall. In reality, the bus was turning, and our sight line didn't se the guard rail. That was in 2007 and reliving this story I can still feel that sensation of thinking we were going over the cliff.

Tell your story with fewer words and more visual aids to help the audience visualize the issue at hand. Think about this for a moment: When you read a novel, you create a picture in your mind based on the words you have read. In your presentation, when you create a picture for the audience, you give them a gift.

When you read a novel, you create a picture in your mind based on the words you have read. In your presentation, when you create a picture for the audience, you give them a gift.

Your Slides Are Your Friend, Not A Crutch

Business audiences expect a slideshow to coincide with your presentation, no matter if you are speaking at a conference or delivering information at a board meeting. Most of these slideshows are developed to be a crutch and not as an aid.

When used properly, your slideshow will act as an aid in helping to get your thoughts and ideas across to your audience. Remember, YOU are the presentation and not your slideshow.

Rate your presentation slide deck by answering these questions:

- Do you pack every word that you want to say on your slides?

- Do you have more bullet points on your slides than bullet holes from the St. Valentine's Day Massacre?
- Are your slides visually appealing to your audience?
- Is your font size is smaller than 32-point?
- Are your charts and graphs confusing because there is too much data on each slide?
- Do you overuse transitions and animations?
- Is the audience reading their email and not looking at your slides?

If you answered *yes* to most of these questions, then your slide deck is a crutch and not an aid.

When acting as an aid, your slides are notecards or a memory jogger; as such, they allow you to create a conversation with the audience. That is the goal.

Here are eight tips to help you create a slideshow that will keep you audience engaged.

1. In many of your slides, eliminate bullet points by using one idea and one picture per slide.
2. When bullet points are warranted for a comparison view, limit the number of bullet points to no more than five.
3. Embed polling questions into your slides to stimulate audience engagement.
4. Use visual aids to help get your key message points across and to create a more engaging experience. Use high quality pictures, images and video, and make them large enough so everyone can see.

5. Choose colors carefully. According to Garr Reynolds, best-selling author and speaker, "Color evokes feelings and color is emotional."[20] Choosing the right colors can help influence the decisions and reactions of the audience. Studies show that color can increase a person's interest and improve their knowledge and retention.

6. Use a font size greater than 32-point, so people in the back of the room can see.

7. Garr Reynolds also suggests that you need to choose your fonts carefully. Fonts communicate subtle messages to your audience, which is why you should think about the fonts you choose. "Comic sans" font would not be preferable in a presentation to the board of directors.

8. Calculate your slides per minute to ensure you are creating a conversation presentation. For example, you are delivering a 60 minute presentation and you have 60 slides, which equates to one-minute per slide. That is too many slides and you have too much content. Heck, you won't have time to even pause. On the other hand, you have 10 slides for the 60 minutes. That is okay if you can talk about the content on each slide for 6 minutes, which seems short, until you realize you are through your slides and there are still 30 minutes to go. I use the metric of between 3 to 5 minutes per slide and use that time to talk about the subject at hand versus reading from the slide.

---

20 Reynolds, Garr, Top Ten Slide Tips, http://www.garrreynolds.com/preso-tips/design/.

One-Idea and One-Picture

I have been weaning myself from a PowerPoint slide filled with text and bullets to the one idea and one picture approach. Remember, it's ultimately all about the audience. What goes through your mind when you see a slide packed with text, numbers, and bullet points? Those slides are not easy on an audience's eyes. Microsoft does not charge you by the number of slides used. Break up the information and put it on multiple slides and add some pictures, video, etc.

Dr. John Molidor, professor of Psychiatry at Michigan State University and past president of the National Speakers Association Board of Directors, taught me something about how the brain responds to PowerPoint slide design. The human brain is divided up into two hemispheres, left and right. The left hemisphere is where language and logic are kept. The right hemisphere is where creativity and the arts are stored. The left side controls the right side of the body and the right side controls the left side of body.

When you develop a PowerPoint slide with the one-idea and one-picture approach, place the picture on the left side of the slide and the text on the right side of the slide. The picture on the left side connects easier with the right hemisphere and the same analogy with the left side. This makes the audiences brain work less and understand more.

However, if the meeting planner needs your slides in advance, consolidate these one-idea and one-picture slides and keep the number of bullet points to a maximum of five. The reason for consolidating the slides is to reduce the amount of printing and copying the meeting planner has to do with your presentation. If the meeting planner is providing them as a downloadable PDF file, still consolidate because it will reduce the file size and make it easier to download. After submitting them, revert to the one-idea and one-picture to a slide approach. This is more work for you and remember it is not about you; it is about your audience and their brains will appreciate your hard work.

Choosing Your Colors and Fonts

Because I believe visual aids are critical to a successful presentation, I want to share more information with you about selecting colors and fonts. Garr Reynolds has great advice on how to choose the colors in your background and in your fonts. In choosing your colors, he suggests that you should know a little bit on color theory, First, colors can be divided into two general categories: cool colors like blue and warm colors like orange. Cool colors work best for backgrounds because they appear to be retreating into the background. Warm colors generally work best for text because they appear better in the foreground. In addition, if you know that you will be presenting in a dark room, use a dark background with white text. However, if the room is well lit, use a white background with dark text.

I have found that in most venues the lights will be somewhere between 75 to 90 percent illuminated. I intentionally design all of my slides with a white background with black font color and a blue thin stripe down the left margin.

You might think that the color selection conversation is a little picky. That won't be the case after we discuss choosing your fonts; now this is picky *and* useful! Reynolds suggests you know and appreciate the difference between a serif font and a sans-serif font. An example of a serif font would be Times New Roman, which has small decorative flourishes at the ends of some of the strokes that make up the letters and numbers, and an example of a sans-serif (without the flourishes) font would be Arial. The original design of the serif fonts was for documents filled with lots of text, like this book. San-serif fonts are better for PowerPoint presentations. You can Google these font types to get an idea of what they look like.

Avoid Copyright Infringement

Let's discuss a critical point about the use of pictures and videos in your presentation: Unless it is a photo or video that you shot or have express permission to use, you could be in violation of copyright. I was accused of a copyright violation once when I got a picture from Google Images and used it in a blog posting. One day, I received a very nasty email informing me that I did not have the rights to use the picture and I needed to remove it from my site and pay a $700 fine, or I would be subject to legal action. After some research, I concluded that it was legit; I paid the penalty and removed the picture. Because pictures help in increasing the audience's retention, I purchased a subscription to Getty Images through istockphoto. com and there are other great options for very low-cost, royalty-free licensed photos, like Adobe Stock. As for videos, you can license stock video from sources like Adobe Stock but if you want to use footage from a movie, you need to buy a license from the Motion Picture Licensing Company (www.mplc.org). Rest assured that there are many ways to find high-quality images and video clips that you can buy affordably (sometimes just $1 a photo), and even sites that provide no-cost images, like Pixabay, Pexels, and Unsplash.

Rehearse Your Presentation to Calculate Your Slide Per Minute

Wait, there is math involved? Yes, and, this is a crucial calculation. One mis-calculation and you complete your presentation too early, or you run out of time and rush through the many slides remaining in your presentation. Either way, this is not very respectful to your audience. It reveals your unpreparedness and lack of professionalism.

For example, you are giving a 60-minute presentation and you have 60 slides, which equates to only one minute per slide (this is easy math to do). One minute per slide is considered "the rapid-fire approach" with no audience participation. You are talking *at* them, not to them. If you have only 10 slides for the 60-minute presentation, then you can create a conversation with your audience for six minutes per slide. Six minutes doesn't seem like a long time until you are giving a presentation and the audience isn't in the conversation mood.

I have learned that the optimum amount of time per slide, at least for the types of presentations I give and the style in which I deliver them, is two to three minutes. That equates to about 20 to 30 slides in your presentation for a 60-minute presentation. However, there is one important and additional step needed. Most of the slides are content driven, but some might contain a video. Determine the length of time of the video and adjust your calculation accordingly. And if you have some audience participation, like an exercise or a quiz/poll, be sure to calculate the time you'll give them to complete those activities.

Don't Lose on A Technicality

Most conferences, especially larger ones, will supply laptop PCs loaded with PowerPoint. If you are a Mac user and can use your laptop, make sure you have all the necessary adapters for VGA, HDMI, or any new type of technology. If you choose to export your Keynote file into PowerPoint, and you have videos embedded with the file extension of .mov, .qt, or .avi, you will need to convert them to .wmv to play them on a laptop PC. Early in my career, I learned this the hard way. I had to use the meeting planner's laptop PC, and my videos would not work. I discovered this only minutes before my presentation was to start and didn't have enough time to delete the slides. Moving forward, I have decided to add Windows 10 and Office 365 to my Mac and develop all my presentations using PowerPoint.

As I stated earlier, YOU are the presentation, not your slideshow, and your slideshow is there simply to aid in the delivery of your message. We have seen way too many bad presentations and now we get scared every time we see another one start. When you use a tool correctly, it helps to aid in your delivery. Just like a screwdriver to a screw. Take the time to plan your presentation slides and be different from most of the presenters out there.

Stop wasting their audience's time and start enhancing their learning experience.

Takeaways

- Design your slides so they are easier on your audience's eyes and brains.
- Avoid copyright infringement by purchasing a subscription to a royalty-free stock photo service where you can license images and video at low cost and/or by using copyright-free images.

- Think about what visual aids to use to help you get your point across.

Knowing Your Audience Better with Seinfeld

> *"Designing a presentation without an audience in mind is like writing a love letter and addressing it 'to whom it may concern.'"*
>
> — Ken Haemer

Demographics matter — when you understand the demographics of your audience, you can better connect with them. This is true in presenting financial information, developing new business, understanding internal and external customers, developing a professional network, and just about every kind of interaction with people. It is inevitable that at some point you will deal with individuals who will not share your views, opinions, or approach. In those instances, you want to quickly assess a person's communication and personality styles so you can adapt, improvise, and keep the conversation moving forward.

There are several tests that can help us understand the personality and communication styles of others, including the popular DiSC® model. This model contains four quadrants that represent parts of the right and left hemispheres of the brain. In general, the left hemisphere is where logic and language reside, and the right hemisphere is where visual and creativity live. The four quadrants of the DiSC® model are Dominance, Influence, Steadiness, and Conscientiousness. Influence and steadiness inhabit the right hemisphere while dominance and conscientiousness inhabit the left hemisphere. The ability to understanding the endearing qualities and the "at their worst" characteristics of each quadrant will help you to better connect with your audience, no matter the situation.

What Seinfeld Quadrant Are You?

I'll let you in on an interesting tidbit: Successful sitcoms often include a character from each quadrant. It is a proven formula because the resulting friction tends to be funny. Next time you watch a sitcom, take note of who is in which quadrant. Seinfeld is a perfect example of this because each of the main characters exemplifies one of the DiSC® quadrants.

Jerry: Dominance

These people are the drivers among us. They are competitive, decisive, independent, determined, and results-oriented. Control and admiration are critical. They also tend to be domineering, impatient, and poor listeners. Disorganization and wasting time drive them crazy. They don't think you should bring your feelings into work. Some people in this category might be considered poor listeners because they often decide independent of input, and anyone else's words are wasting precious oxygen. In fact, sometimes they are described as bullies. People who fit this quadrant are CEOs, CFOs, Managing Partners, Mark Cuban, and General Colin Powell. Their endearing quality is their ability to get things done and take charge. At their worst, they are very poor listeners.

Elaine: Influence

These are the cheerleader types who want to do what they love without being confused by the facts. They are optimistic, animated, persuasive, imaginative, enthusiastic, excellent communicators who enjoy telling stories. Often described as dreamers and very creative, they love having fun, being the center of attention, and receiving applause. However, they tend to talk too much, overwhelming others with information, and they have short attention spans. Structure frustrates them. People who fit this quadrant are salespeople, speakers, and coaches, like Coach Boone in the movie "Remember the Titans." Their endearing quality is that they are good communicators and visionaries. At their worst, they tend to be disorganized and miss deadlines.

Kramer: Steadiness

These are the "can't we all just get along and work together" people who want to be sure that everyone is okay. They are friendly, reliable, and supportive, like a Labrador Retriever. Patient and very diplomatic, they want everyone to like them and obsess if someone doesn't. They are very concerned about personal relationships and harmony in the workplace but tend to be overly sensitive, conformist, and lacking in time boundaries. Rather than tell you what they think, they will say what you want to hear (which can be a dangerous trait). They don't like to be rushed, don't want to be alone, and avoid conflict when possible. People who fit this quadrant are human resources professionals, therapists, and clergy, like Pope Francis and Carl Jung. Their endearing quality is they understand diplomacy and demonstrate patience. At their worst, they tend to be indecisive, easily overwhelmed, and miss deadlines.

George: Conscientiousness

These are the thinkers. Efficient, thorough, accurate, and careful, they want to get it right every time. They are disciplined and love solving problems and researching issues. This group tends to be very critical and picky. They don't like disorganization or surprises. People who fit this quadrant are accountants, engineers, actuaries, and the character Sheldon Cooper from the "Big Bang Theory" sitcom. Their endearing quality is that they love detail and research. At their worst, they are rigid, argumentative, and stubborn.

Understanding Your Sitcom Cast

Now that you understand the quadrants, you can begin to think about how to work and respond to any cast of characters in your organization and in your audience. Friction will naturally arise because these are people with different outlooks. Still, you must tailor your conversation to meet a particular group communication style or to an audience that contains all types, like a company quarterly briefing or a board meeting. So, how do we connect and adapt to groups that are not like us?

To connect with those who are in the **dominant quadrant**, be direct, be specific, and offer multiple solutions. Remember, they are the deciders. If you give them only one option, it's more than likely going to fail, or it can become their idea instead of yours.

To connect with those who are in the **influence quadrant**, be enthusiastic and positive, and avoid details. Put things in a way that they can understand. Tell them a story versus spewing data at them. I have often heard accountants complain that the salespeople never get their expense reports in on time. My solution would be to point out to those salespeople that they file early for their tax refund so that the government doesn't get to use their money any longer than necessary, so they should submit their expense report to the company for a similar reason.

To connect with those who are in the **steadiness quadrant**, engage in small talk, ask a lot of questions, and be informal, as if speaking with a friend. Just don't let them suck away your time and extend your workday. You need to be respectful but firm about managing the conversation. Let them know you appreciate chatting, but it's time to get down to business.

And for those who are in the **conscientiousness quadrant**, provide them with only the detail that they need to help make the decision and refrain from telling them a story. The more precise information (which contains numbers and spreadsheets) you give them, the happier they are.

Having positive experiences with people from all backgrounds and perspectives starts with respect. Respect comes from having a better understanding of who people really are and embracing the type of personality and communication style they possess. Just like in improv, communication goes two ways, so the better we understand others — including their pet peeves and their hot buttons, their likes and dislikes — the better we will get along and can feed off one another. It always comes back to listening carefully to what people need and want, adapting readily to the situation, and taking your agenda off the table.

Takeaways

- Try to gain an understanding of the audience by using this back-of-the envelope approach to the DiSC®.

- Those who are more gregarious, creative, and visionary, remember "don't confuse them with the details and facts." Tell them a story instead.

- The more that you respect your audience, the better you will know them.

The Four Stages of Competence

"It's not uncommon for people to overvalue the importance of demonstrating their competence and power, often at the expense of demonstrating their warmth."

— Amy Cuddy

Before developing a presentation, you need to know your audience and have at least a general sense of the baseline for their current understanding of your topic. Try to determine what level of competence the audience possesses because it will have an impact on how you structure and deliver your presentation. I remember once when I was a staff accountant that one of the senior managers was trying to explain a complicated concept to me. I just couldn't quite grasp what he was talking about. My technical knowledge was not at his level, and he was not communicating with me at a level of my understanding. Both of us left that conversation frustrated. I didn't speak up to tell him I needed him to explain the basics (probably because I was embarrassed) and he didn't offer the basics (probably because he didn't want to come off as condescending).

So let's talk about how audience competence should guide your presentation strategy. Many people might know the "four stages of competence" model developed in the 1970s at Gordon Training

International, a well-respected education and training consultancy. As a point of reference, this competency model has been attributed to Abraham Maslow, but has not been found in any of his work.

Here is *my* version of the Gordon Training International four stages of competence:

1. **I don't know what I don't know, you know.**

   A person at this level of competence might be a new employee who recently graduated with a degree in accounting. They may have taken an auditing class, but they don't know how to audit. They may have taken a taxation course, but they do not know all the complexities of tax law. The person just doesn't recognize that there is a gap between what they know and what they need to know. The only way to move to the next level is for them to recognize their incompetence to the skill and have the desire to acquire the knowledge to master it.

2. **I don't know, and I want to learn.**

   When someone begins to increase their standard of competence through repetition and practice, they move into this level. They know that making mistakes and errors is integral to this learning process. For example, the new associate is learning about the auditing process by learning how to reconcile bank statements and receive feedback on their work. Feedback is critical in the learning process but when taken too personally can bruise some egos. That can create a negative mindset if not presented properly. It is the responsibility of the supervisor to deliver feedback in a positive light to avoid the negative mindset.

3. **Getting closer to becoming a master.**

Now the individual begins to have a deeper understanding of the skill necessary and can execute to it with minimal errors. They have acquired the skills to be competent in their current role and have shown the ability to continue learning. It's at this level where they may be a candidate for promotion.

In the advancement process, part of the individual's skill will revert back to #1. Perhaps they are promoted on their increased technical knowledge but are still lacking the skills to manage a group of people. As when they were at the first phase of competency, suddenly they don't know what they don't know again. From previous experience, they should recognize this new knowledge gap and begin the process of closing it. Mastering each knowledge gap will help them accelerate to the next level.

4. **Ultimate Master Yoda!**

At this level, the person has extensive exposure to multiple facets of the business and, through practice, the skills needed to succeed are second nature to them. I tend to equate this to the job positions of chief financial officer, a partner in a firm, or chief executive officer. With extensive depth and breadth of knowledge, solving issues becomes more intuitive. The lessons learned along the way are a point of reference for finding solutions.

Here's another example I like to use: a golfer. The ultimate master Yoda golfer is the one who is currently on the PGA or LPGA tour. They don't have to think about the basics of golf: stance, grip, swing, etc. They visualize the shot, consider all variables, then just swing the golf club with perfect tempo and rhythm, hitting the ball almost to perfection. Well, most of the time. They maintain this level of excellence with consistent practice, and that is the key to remaining unconsciously competent. Without regular practice, the person will drop back to the third stage.

Understanding your audience's level of competence allows you to tailor your presentation to meet or slightly exceed the audience's level of expertise. That alignment of what they know and what you are sharing allows you to create a conversation with the audience. When you connect with the group they are more likely to retain you message and be able to act on it. However, if we are talking about complex issues to which the audience cannot relate, all we are doing is just talking over their heads.

That alignment of what they know and what you are sharing allows you to create a conversation with the audience.

We've all been in presentations where the presenter delivers highly technical information, using insider jargon and unrecognizable acronyms. The audience members have deer-in-the-headlights looks, and are not engaged with the speaker, let alone having a conversation. Tailor your presentations to meet the competency level of the learner. As a result, you'll have greater success in connecting with them and raising their level of retention.

Takeaways

- Determine your audience's current level of competence and compare it to yours.

- Understanding your audience's level of competence allows you to tailor your presentation to meet or slightly exceed the audience's level of expertise.

- This will help you connect better with your team, your organization, and to your audiences.

Chapter 13

STEP #3 OF BEING AMAZING AND ENGAGING – PREPARING FOR YOUR PRESENTATION

> *"Many attempts to communicate are nullified by saying too much."*
>
> — Robert Greenleaf

Creating a Conversation Experience Presentation

You have finished writing your presentation and now it is time to practice. I am frequently asked if presenters should memorize their entire presentation word-for-word or should just wing it, a.k.a improvise? The answer depends on two things: your personal preference with a scripted presentation and your level of experience as a presenter.

There are two types of presenters: those who use PowerPoint and those who don't. For those who don't, memorizing your speech is a must and I discuss ways of memorizing in the next chapter.

However, one of the pitfalls to memorizing your presentation is human error. When you make a mistake — and you will — it's easy to get flustered if you feel it breaks up a flawless "performance" of a script. You may forget a word, or many words, or even a paragraph. Now your focus is on the mistake, not the audience or the content, and you may freak out a bit. When you start to panic, and your nerves are jumping everywhere, there may be unexpected side effects, and a big one is the Dreaded Shallow Breather Syndrome (DSBS). You can forget to breathe! When you fail to properly inhale and exhale, your brain doesn't receive enough oxygen. A lack of oxygen leads to memory loss, and that ultimately can derail your presentation. If you experience DSBS, just pause and take a few deep breaths. Smile. This should help you get back on track. If not, then own it. Tell the audience you just had a "brain cloud," look at your notes, and carry on. It's human to say, "You know what? I feel like I'm forgetting something important that I want to share with you so I'm going to glance at my notes to ensure you get your money's worth."

For those who use PowerPoint, you still need to put in time learning your presentation. You may have all the information inside of your head but if you can't access it in a logical way to get your point across; you will come off unprepared, scatter-brained, and, sadly, just a rambling mess. All your credibility is now gone.

PowerPoint slides are nothing more than giant index cards to help jog your memory. I find that memorizing my presentation about 80% allows me the flexibility to insert anything new that would be relevant to the conversation. As outlined earlier in this book, if you structure your slides with one topic and one picture, and show up well-rehearsed, you will create that conversation experience and have a strong connection with the audience.

PowerPoint slides are nothing more than giant index cards to help jog your memory.

A challenge that can throw you off your game comes when questions are asked. You will not be perceived as the subject-matter expert if you struggle in answering questions or don't appear confident in your answers. To avoid this and keep the conversation moving forward, try to anticipate what questions could be asked and research the answers long before your presentation. In undertaking this process, ask your boss and fellow subject matter experts what questions you should anticipate.

The level of mastery in delivering a presentation is when you can navigate the message, insert relevant stories from you inventory, and engage with the audience by asking questions and giving answers, and not break a sweat. I call this the level of improvisation.

One gets to this level by delivering the same presentation repeatedly, so that it becomes second nature. This takes a lot of work, time, and confidence in your skills.

For example, when I first taught beginning accounting at the university level, I put in hundreds of hours to make sure I understood the material inside and out. It wasn't until the start of my fourth year teaching the same subject that I was able to begin to use the improvisation technique. I slowly instituted this method, but only for a couple of chapters where I had a high comfort level. After a couple more years, I was well-versed on the content, and I could anticipate and react to student's questions. I created a conversation in the classroom versus a lecture. Toward the end of my college teaching career, I was the subject matter expert, and the improvisation technique was my standard for that class. Lucky for me, it didn't matter if a new edition textbook came out — beginning accounting has not changed very much over the years.

The goal of any presentation is to create a conversation with your audience versus a classroom lecture. Think back to your days in school when you had to listen to an instructor robotically drone on about a subject. That memory alone should be enough inspiration for you to work hard in creating the conversation experience! Creating that conversation experience will allow you to better connect with your audience, increase your standing as the subject matter expert, and improve the audience's retention of the information you are delivering.

Takeaways

- Determine what type of presentation you are preparing for — with or without PowerPoint.

- Avoid the DSBS and breathe.

- It takes a lot of hard work to achieve the level of improvisation. Keep practicing and keep the faith.

Two Memory Techniques to Help Create a Conversation Experience

"I should remember more, and I have a pretty good memory."

— Cesar Romero

There are critical achievements that all professional speakers share. You want to be recognized as a subject matter expert in your field. You also want to be seen as a polished speaker who creates a "conversation experience" and connects with every person in your audience. You want to be the best, and you can achieve those goals. But you need a strategy. One of the strongest techniques for creating conversation experiences with audiences is a form of memorization.

You want to be the best, and you can achieve those goals. But you need a strategy.

I don't mean memorizing your entire presentation, repeating it verbatim, or reading from a slide presentation. This strategy does involve some actual memorization but also visualization and memory triggers. *Fair warning: This technique takes practice.*

To begin to learn this technique, write the opening and closing paragraphs for your presentation. They must be meaningful for your audience. You want to grab their attention in the beginning and offer a call-to-action when you close. Think about what pain points your audience is experiencing and what solution you are providing them to solve these issues. This should not be difficult if you have spent time gaining a better understanding of your audience.

Then memorize those two paragraphs word-for-word. Practice them until you can deliver them perfectly. Knowing your opening paragraph by heart can help calm your nerves, which helps increase your level of confidence. Memorizing your closing paragraph will help you "stick the landing" and end your presentation on a high note. Your call-to-action is the key message point — the seed you have been planting throughout your presentation. You want the audience to remember it, and act on it.

Knowing your opening paragraph by heart can help calm your nerves, which helps increase your level of confidence. Memorizing your closing paragraph will help you "stick the landing" and end your presentation on a high note.

Now it's time to learn and incorporate an advanced memory technique. The method that many speakers use is called the memory blueprint and includes the use of cues. We all have used a variety of cues to learn new and complex things. Who doesn't remember learning the alphabet by singing the ABCs? That's a cue and it is the way you are going to create your memory blueprint.

The memory blueprint is an imaginary location in your mind where you can store these cues. The most common type of memory system is called a memory palace. This is thinking of a familiar place – your home "palace" and placing nuggets of information you want to remember in different rooms of your home. Now take an imaginary trip through your house, taking the same path each and every time, stopping in each room to see the nuggets you left behind about what you want to say. After you are done, off to the next room. It sounds more difficult than it is.

Here is how to build your memory blueprint.

1. Think about your house, apartment, or office building for your memory blueprint. Personally, I find that using my home's design is the best — I have lived in the same house for more than 20

years. I am very familiar with the layout and navigating through the house is intuitive, I don't have to think about it. Draw your blueprint on a piece of paper showing all the major rooms, entries, and exits. You will add details to this blueprint as you develop your palace.

2. Look at your blueprint and decide on the route you will take every time from beginning to end.

3. Now memorize the route you will consistently take. For example, I start by walking in the front door then taking a right turn and walking into the living room, then take a left turn and walking into the dining room, then taking another left turn into the kitchen walking straight from the kitchen to the family room, then turning around leaving the family room, and now taking a left walking out my back door.

4. Place one presentation key point in each particular location in your memory palace; actually, write that point on your blueprint. Then list two words that are specific details related to your key points in each location.

5. Create a mental image of each of your key points and over exaggerate them by creating picture to help in memorization. I exaggerate the key point of Cursed with Knowledge with a picture of a witch doctor deep in the jungle, chanting over a boiling pot while adding eye of newt, in with carrots, and a bottle of bourbon – bottle and all, raising her arms to the sky and her chanting gets louder and louder.

6. Then begin to practice by visualizing your path through your memory palace and bring in your cues to memorize the list. Many practice runs will be needed to train your memory and capture your entire presentation.

SAMPLE MEMORY BLUEPRINT

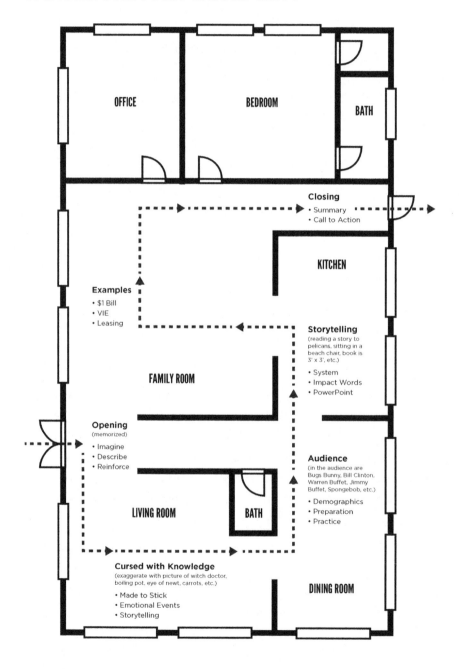

Put these two memorization methods — memorizing your intro and closing and then creating a memory blueprint — together and run through your presentation. Your opening paragraph is represented by the front door, and your closing paragraph is where you exit the building. When you visualize your path through the building, think about the mnemonic memory of the key points and what you want to say about them. Practice your presentation using this method until you are comfortably moving from the entry to the exit. Keep your blueprint handy as a reference tool so you stay on the planned route through your memory palace.

The day of your presentation, take your written memory blueprint with you, and put it in a place where only you can see it, maybe on a podium. Use it as a backup plan to keep you on track, just in case you forget where you are in your presentation.

You many need to invest a considerable amount of time to get comfortable with the memory palace method but there is a big payoff: You can move from a lecturer to a conversational presenter.

Takeaways

- Memorize your opening paragraph to calm your nerves and be able to walk through the "front door" and make a powerful entrance.

- Memorize your closing paragraph and deliver a moving call-to-action.

- Take time to build your blueprint and remember to deliver it taking the same route each and every time.

Practice! Are We Talking About Practice?

"Spectacular achievement is always preceded by unspectacular preparation."

— Robert H. Schuller

It was 2002, and I can still hear former NBA Allen Iverson's classic rant to the media, "I'm supposed to be the franchise player, and we in here talking about practice. I mean, listen: We talking about practice." Allen didn't want to practice because he felt that his past accomplishments (NBA Rookie of the Year in 1997, NBA All Star and League Most Valuable Player in 2001) gave him the privilege to just show up on game day and play.

The professionals who I follow, whether they are athletes, speakers, or leaders, don't follow the Allen Iverson methodology of practice because they do not want to be complacent and lose their precision and edge.

When I was Program Chair of Accounting at Franklin University, part of my job was to hire adjunct facility. When a new faculty member with little to no previous teaching experience joined the staff, I would sit down and discuss the amount of preparation and practice they would need to be successful in the classroom. I would describe this by saying, "We are paying you $2,500 for the course and because this is your first time teaching, that will equate to about a nickel per hour." The look of horror on their face was sobering. They needed to comprehend that they would need to understand the material inside and out, demonstrate the homework assignments, and answer questions, even for an introductory course in accounting. In the classroom, they needed to be perceived as the subject-matter-expert, and this was achieved not through lecture, but through conversations discussing the material. I had to convince each new faculty member that he or she spoke a foreign language —accounting — and their role was to develop a way to translate the accounting language to plain English. Translating accounting into plain English takes a lot of practice.

Translating accounting into plain English takes a lot of practice.

If they were successful, then they would have the opportunity to teach the same course repeatedly to gain that proficiency, which in turn reduced prep time and drove the salary per hour higher. Practice!

Practicing is extremely important, and I want to revisit and go into more depth about Chapter 11's exploration of Getting Past Your Fear of Public Speaking.

Practicing in front of a mirror, I always ask, "Is that how you will be presenting to your audience, in front of a mirror?" Of course not. You won't be looking at yourself ... you'll be looking at your audience. The premise is valid, to see yourself and the mannerisms you are projecting. However, wouldn't it be better if you practiced your presentation in front of a video camera and then watched yourself later? "YIKES! You want me to watch myself?! I hate watching myself on camera." *Really?* You can't stand the idea of watching yourself on camera, but you want everyone in your audience to have to watch you. That is not congruent. And it's honestly not fair.

I understand the discomfort watching a recording of your presentation because I hated it, too. I find that practicing in front of a camera and pretending that I am delivering my presentation to an audience is the second-best way of becoming proficient. Even better, record your performance while you are delivering it to a live audience. Then watch it a couple days later. Either way, you will discover more areas that need improvement than you would with any other way of practicing. The camera never lies.

Early in my career, I practiced by reviewing my presentation slides while sitting at my desk, only hearing the words in my head. But that didn't help me gain the full experience, and I don't suggest that technique. Outside of a panel discussion, a clear majority of presentations are given standing up, and all require the use of "outside words" words. My suggestion is to find a conference or training room that has a projector, then plug in your slide deck and practice out loud. This method helps you to hear the words and decide if there are better words to use or a different way of expressing your thoughts.

I am often asked "how much practice is enough?" Let me paint a picture: You are going deliver a 60-minute conference presentation. Just before you start, your computer freezes, and now you can't use PowerPoint. Can you give your presentation with 90% accuracy without the use of your slides? When you can honestly say *yes*, then you are well rehearsed.

Here's another scenario: You are going to deliver a presentation to a board of directors. No visual aids, no PowerPoint, just you. Can you give your talk without referring to your notes? Can you anticipate questions that will be asked, and are you able to answer them without reference to any notes? Once again, when you can honestly say *yes*, then you are well rehearsed.

Another practice technique that I use is to *visualize* my entire presentation. This method is like what athletes do before they play or compete. They see themselves hitting the shot, fielding the ball, making the putt. I want to visualize the entire room, stage, audience, and envision myself as I deliver my presentation.

I utilized this technique when I gave a keynote address entitled 'Embrace Your Inner Superhero.' I began visualizing the presentation two weeks before the presentation date. I knew there would be about 150 attendees, the event would be held at a hotel conference room, and I had 75 minutes. Having presented many times in similar settings, I knew how the room would be set up with round tables, a stage with a podium, and two large screens on either side of the stage.

I would visualize my entire presentation from my introduction to me walking on to the stage to delivering my speech. It's easy to visualize a perfect performance but that would not help me get past obstacles. In addition to visualizing the actual material, I visualized problems, lots of problems. I saw myself stumble over certain words, saw me stumbling around the podium, even saw me taking a wrong step and falling off the stage. I would do this visualization countless times to begin to work out the kinks, all to ensure that I would not stumble on words or off the stage. The day of the presentation I had rehearsed all aspects of my keynote 50 or more times, and that does not include the number of hours of working with the material and vocalizing the speech. I was ready. And there were no stumbles.

If you want to feel comfortable and be a better speaker, presenter, trainer, or facilitator, you need to put in the practice time. By the way, no matter how busy you are, there is always time to practice, even if it is only 5 to 10 minutes. You can always find a place to practice, whether it is in the shower, on your daily commute, or in your kitchen in front of your pets. I admit that I do practice in front of my two Labrador retrievers a lot. I set up the video camera and present to my attentive audience using my "outside words." Then I watch the video and critique my performance.

You can always find a place to practice, whether it is in the shower, on your daily commute, or in your kitchen in front of your pets.

Takeaways

- Embrace practice and don't be like Allen Iverson.

- Practice should take place in a training or conference room, not in front of a mirror.

- Record you practice session and then watch it to find the flaws.

To Be the Best, Watch the Best

"Good is to a presentation like fine is to a compliment. Your purpose is to make something happen!"

— Karen Hough, author of *Be the Best Bad Presenter Ever*

As a speaker, presenter or facilitator, we are always honing our craft. Making subtle changes and improvements in our delivery, stage persona, or our body language is key to developing a professional presentation. I have learned that if I want to be the best, I must go watch the best. Learn from them but don't mimic them. Stay authentic to yourself and use what you learned to become one of the best. I took that piece of advice to heart and spent countless hours watching past U.S. Presidents, speakers at the NSA Annual Convention and at our local NSA chapter meetings, and TED Talks.

Former U.S. Presidents Ronald Reagan, Bill Clinton, and Barack Obama were known for their incredible speaking skills. They knew how to connect with an audience and capture their imagination. Watch and listen to their cadence and tone of voice. Listen for when they pause and then observe the look on their faces. Watch what they do with their hands. Early in Bill Clinton's political career, when he would speak, he had the tendency to point his finger at the audience. He was given advice to stop pointing his finger because it makes the audience defensive. Instead of pointing his finger, he would make a fist and place his thumb on top of his fist and make the pointing gesture without using his finger. I have heard this method to be called the "remote control."

As a member of the National Speakers Association, you gain access to some of the best speakers, both domestically and internationally — like Mike Rayburn, Patricia Fripp, and Derrick Kayongo. When I see them on stage, I am constantly studying their mannerisms, pace, voice, delivery — all the nuances that work together to create a powerful presentation.

The next time you can observe a professional speaker, pull out your note pad and take some notes. What movements are they using on stage? How do they connect with the audience? Try to capture their body language, use of humor, design of their presentation slides, use of the microphone, fluctuation in their voice, and their eye contact with the audience. Write it all down.

Another way to study excellent presenters is to watch some TED Talks. If you are unfamiliar with them, go to www.TED.com and read their history. The short version is that TED stands for Technology, Entertainment, and Design because the tradition of the talks was born from a conference with this overarching theme. Today, it is so much more. TED Talks are presentations averaging 18 minutes on nearly any topic so long as it contains a valuable message in the tradition of "ideas worth sharing." Some notable TED Talk speakers include Bill Gates, Al Gore, and Tony Robbins, to name just a few.

For as long as I have been watching TED Talks, the top five TED talks have been:

1. Sir Kenneth Robinson – Do Schools Kill Creativity?
2. Amy Cuddy – Your Body Language May Shape Who You Are
3. Simon Sinek – How Great Leaders Inspire Action
4. Brené Brown – The Power of Vulnerability
5. Mary Roach – 10 Things You Didn't Know About Orgasm

When you study TED Talks, remember this: These speakers are taking very complex information and presenting it through stories and visual aids. No TED Talk is ever a data dump. They are evoking an emotion in the audience, whether it is laughter, sadness, or shock. If they can do this, I am sure you can, too. It does require a lot of work but in the end, you'll have a presentation worthy of sharing.

Go to my landing page www.takingthenumboutofthenumbersbook. com and click on the links to watch The Best of Ronald Reagan and watch him deliver his humor with perfection. Watch "Bill Clinton Bids Farewell at the 2000 White House Correspondents' Dinner" and watch his facial expressions, especially when he is discussing writing his resume. Watch a clip from President Obama's 2015 Correspondents' Dinner titled "President Obama's Anger Translator" and watch his timing and delivery. Finally, watch one TED Talk a week, any one — just watch and study.

You want to *be* the best? Go watch the best and become a member of the National Speakers Association. The National Speakers Association is the most recognized and respected professional speakers' organization in the industry. It is well worth your investment if you want to strive to become one of the best, no matter your area of expertise.

Takeaways

- To be the best, watch the best.
- To be the best, watch the best.
- To be the best, watch the best.

Being Authentic

"You attract the right things when you have a sense of who you are."

— Amy Poehler

When I used to deliver technical accounting seminars and conference breakout sessions, my evaluations always exceeded 4.5 on a 5-point scale. I earned these scores by being engaging, well-rehearsed, and knowledgeable on the topic. But something was missing. I would get a lot of CPAs coming up to me afterwards and thanking me for one of the best presentations on a boring accounting topic. You would think that would be sustainable in growing a speaking business. But it wasn't … because something was missing.

How do we demonstrate our true nature and our beliefs to another person? Passion!

How do we demonstrate our true nature and our beliefs to another person? Passion! That's one of the ways that we show our authenticity. Along with passion about our subject, we must be able to articulate it concisely that our audiences can understand. To achieve this, we must spend time developing the content and practicing our delivery.

That is what was missing. I wasn't *passionate* about the new revenue recognition or leasing standard. What I was passionate about was how improvisation is a leadership tool and how it can change your life and your business.

There is one key component that must exist along with content and practice to be deemed authentic. That key ingredient is our body language. Think of it this way. Have you ever witnessed a presentation during which the presenter appeared less than 100% confident with the material? They may be passionate about the topic, but they are unprepared. Now think of the person's body language and what is projected to the audience. You are probably seeing the presenter's body in a closed and defensive posture. Their arms are close to their trunk and chest, or they may be even crossing their arms across their chest.

In the *Harvard Business Review* article "How to Become an Authentic Speaker," author Nick Morgan lays out four steps to becoming a more authentic speaker.[21]

1. **Be open with the audience.**

   When we are open with our audiences, our hands and arms are away from the midsection of our body, and our palms are open upward. This is a sign of being truthful. When we begin to speak more comfortably, our body language is communicating to the audience that we are confident in the message that we are delivering.

2. **Connect with the audience.**

   To connect with your audience fully, you must eliminate barriers and use your voice. If you are well rehearsed and confident, then stepping away from the podium and stepping closer to the audience helps in this connection. By making eye contact, smiling, and modulating your tone of voice, you will further connect with the audience.

3. **Bring the passion.**

   Let your emotion come through your voice and your movements. As I've suggested before, view a few TED Talks and watch how these presenters bring the passion into the presentation. If you want to be the best, you need to watch the best.

4. **Listen to your audience.**

   To do this, we need to listen with our ears and eyes. Observe your audience's body language. What are they telling you? For

---

21 Morgan, Nick, "How to Become an Authentic Speaker," *Harvard Business Review*, https://hbr.org/2008/11/how-to-become-an-authentic-speaker.

example, during your presentation, you may notice many of the audience members have their arms crossed over their chest in a very defensive manner. What is it telling you? It's telling you that you've said something that upset them, and you need to diffuse the situation. Another example would be that your audience has that sleepy deer-in-the-headlights look. That should tell you that you are not connecting with them at all and you need to change it up to re-engage that audience. An engaged audience is slightly leaning forward, listening intently, nodding their heads, and not reading their email.

Ultimately, being more authentic requires being the subject matter expert who is well rehearsed and confident with the material. It requires being able to apply Morgan's four steps of authenticity both physically and emotionally. This takes a lot of time and practice in front of a live audience. Keep these steps in mind during your next presentation and, over time, you will be perceived as being a truly *authentic* speaker.

Takeaways

- Learn from the best but be yourself.
- Show the audience how passionate you are about your subject.
- Be well rehearsed and confident.

Chapter 14

STEP #4 OF BEING AMAZING AND ENGAGING – DELIVERING YOUR PRESENTATION

> *"The goal of effective communication should be for listeners to say 'Me too!' versus 'So what?'"*
>
> — Jim Rohn

Seven Platform Tips for Connecting with Your Audience

I was delivering a presentation once and wanted to test out some new technology. There was an app on my cell phone that I could use to advance the slide deck. How cool was that? I thought the audience would think it was a cool tool. It wasn't as sexy as I thought because I never told the audience why I had my cell phone in my hand. They thought I was waiting for an urgent phone call and were not totally engaged in my presentation. I know this because after the presentation some people asked me why I kept the phone in my hand — *they wondered if my wife expecting!* I had inadvertently become a distraction to the audience because their focus was on my phone and not my words.

Here are seven platform considerations for helping you become a better presenter and less of a distraction.

1. Podium or No Podium

Do you like to use a podium when delivering your presentation or do you like to be able to walk around? For those of you who like the podium, is it because it creates a buffer from the audience or it is easier to refer to your notes or script? For those of you who like to walk around, how comfortable are you delivering a presentation from behind a podium?

Personally, I prefer to walk around and stay as far away from the podium as possible. I did have to deliver one speech from a podium, and it was very uncomfortable. I don't like to read from a script, but in this instance, I had a final draft of a speech delivered to me about an hour before the presentation. This speech had some edits, and I was unable to get familiar with the content. I was extremely uncomfortable, and you could tell by my voice and body language.

2. Hands

"What to do with those pesky hands?" It's one of my favorite questions, and I get asked it all the time. Do you let them hang by your side? Do you clasp and unclasp them throughout your presentation? The one thing you *shouldn't* do is to put them into your pants pockets because it looks unprofessional. Let your hands be part of your presentation to add additional visualization to your point. But be careful of the large, exaggerated hand and arm gestures. You don't want to look like you're trying to hail a New York City cab or be rescued from a deserted island. When you practice, keep your hands below an imaginary line just below your chest. Use gestures to enhance your presentation without being a distraction.

3. Remember to Smile

When you smile, it looks like you are enjoying yourself and having fun. It is also more engaging to the audience. Think about this — when you watch a presentation, do you connect more to a speaker who is smiling rather than one who is frowning or not showing any emotion? Smiling wins! However, we will all have "one of those days" when finding a smile is about as likely as winning the lottery.

How do you give an honest smile when you don't feel like it? My coach in New York offered great advice. He said that when you need a smile, all you must do is say three words in your head: "I love you," but said in a southern accent. You read that correctly. It's an excellent way to get a smile when you need one. A smile goes a long way to helping you and your audience relax and engage. Remember, the "I love you" exercise uses inside words, not outside words! No need to be saying that out loud.

4. Don't Immediately Start Your Presentation

Your introduction has concluded. Go to the middle of the stage, pause for a second or two, then begin your presentation. Give the audience a chance to see you before you begin. Let them get familiar with you — you want them to get to know you a bit, to trust you. It isn't easy to slow things down. Your body is highly charged with adrenaline, and you want to get started quickly. No need to come flying onto the stage like Kramer and screeching to an awkward halt, all the while bursting with the first few lines of your presentation! Don't be jarring to the audience when the idea is to let them welcome you to the stage.

You need to slow the adrenaline high and you can do this by taking two or three deep breaths. This will help relax your nerves and calm down the excitement you feel. If you are off stage and the audience can't see you, then bend at the waist and breathe deeply for a moment or two. While doing this, think about slowing your inner clock down to a leisurely pace. Now you can confidently walk to the middle of the stage, pause for a moment, and begin.

5. Moving on Stage

Have you ever been to an amusement park that has those games of skill where you can win a big stuffed animal? One of the games I remember is a shooting gallery. The objects are in constant movement while the person is aiming at the object. That constant movement distracts you as you focus on the target. When you are like that on stage, you become a pacer. If you pace back and forth on stage like a caged lion, it is because your adrenaline is over-flowing or your nerves are on high alert. Or even worse, you have not prepared enough. Breathing, just like we talked about before, helps keep you calm, confident, and can prevent pacing.

It's nice to move around the stage but when you have a point to make, stop, plant, and deliver. When you stop and plant, it tells the audience that what you are about to say is important, and they need to give you their full attention. You don't have to stop, plant, and deliver in the middle of the stage all the time. You can be stage right or stage left and address the critical point. Move toward the stage area you have selected, slow down your step and maintain eye contact with the audience. Then plant and deliver.

6. The Pause

A pause is a powerful tool for every presenter. The pause can be used just before delivering a punchline, or for dramatic effect, or to let the audience catch up and process what they have heard. It can also be used just to give yourself a quick moment to gather your thoughts. Many new presenters start their presentation at a fast pace and never slow down. That is due to nerves or possibly the lack of preparation.

As you practice, practice where you will put the pauses. Feel the beat of the pause and imagine the faces of the audience when they have that AHA! moment or the look they have just before you hit them with the punchline.

7. Eye Contact

Make eye contact with the audience. You don't have to stare them down and make them feel uncomfortable. But you shouldn't be focused over the heads to the back of the room or looking down at your shoes. Just make quick eye contact with attendees across the room. If they are smiling and looking back at you, you know they are engaged. If they look angry, are sleeping, are reading their email, or are demonstrating negative body language, you need to a find way to adjust your presentation and change the atmosphere in the room. Connect with your audience to pick up on the clues they are sending.

Work on these tips and techniques every time you are presenting. The one that I struggled with early on was pacing. I didn't realize I was a pacer until I watched the video of my presentation. The next time I did a presentation, I kept in the back of my mind: Slow down, quit pacing, don't be a distraction.

There is so much that we must be aware of on top of our technical knowledge when we are presenting. The best presenters know that a subject-matter expert is not the same as an expert presenter. They work hard to improve all presentation skills so they can be more engaging with their audiences.

The best presenters know that a subject-matter expert is not the same as an expert presenter.

Takeaways

- Remember to smile at the start, during, and the end of your presentation.
- Let the audience get to know you for a few seconds before you begin.
- There is power in the pause.

Inhaling and Exhaling is Key in Public Speaking

"Your voice is worthwhile. Have faith in it."

— John Lasseter

The most important thing to do when you give a presentation is to breathe. That may sound like an obvious statement, but when presenting to a group it is easy to forget to breathe properly. When you forget to take good, deep breaths, your lungs can run out of air before you finish a sentence, then your voice becomes soft and even crackles. An acting coach I worked with in New York referred to this as the "shallow breathing syndrome" — what I call the "dreaded shallow breather syndrome" in Chapter 13 of this book.

Think about this way, if you are a shallow breather, and the most important point you want to convey to the audience comes at the end of a sentence, it is going to fall flat and limp, just like the dreaded dead fish handshake. Without sufficient supply of oxygen in your lungs, your voice cannot project to the back of the audience, showing confidence and a command of the stage.

According to a *Harvard Business Review* article by Allison Shapira, "Breathing Is the Key to Persuasive Public Speaking," deep breathing exercises help to harness the power of breathing to speak with confidence and electricity.[22] Here is a deep breathing exercise that will help rid shallow breathing.

- Stand straight, shoulders back, and chest out.
- Now take a deep breath through your nose by expanding your stomach and not your chest.
- Then begin to let out all of the air slowly through your mouth and squeeze every last air molecule out of your lungs.
- Repeat the exercise again and again and again.

Once you are comfortable doing that, take the exercise to the next level.

- This time when you exhale, slowly count: "1 ... 2 ... 3 ... 4 ... 5 ..."

---

22 Shapira, Allison, "Breathing is the Key to Persuasive Public Speaking," *Harvard Business Review*, June 30, 2015, https://hbr.org/2015/06/breathing-is-the-key-to-persuasive-public-speaking.

- Master that and take it to an even level higher: Exhale saying the words, "Do Re Me Fa So La Ti Do."
- As you practice and gain confidence, add more words like, "Hello, my name is [insert name]."

Caution! When doing this exercise for the first time, if you begin to feel lightheaded, stop and try another time until you get your stamina up — your lungs need to adapt to this technique. Once you have your stamina up, do 10 reps, four times a day for a month. You should see improved results almost overnight. Even when you do not have a presentation scheduled, practice every day. You can back down to 10 reps each day you are not speaking. On presentation days, shoot for 20 reps.

In addition to what proper breathing does to strengthen your voice, proper breathing helps to keep sufficient oxygen in your blood and your brain. Having sufficient oxygen helps you focus on your presentation. Oxygenated brains are sharp brains!

What happens when you blank out and can't remember what you were going to say next? You probably stand there with all of those eyes staring at you, and you begin to panic. When we panic on stage, what do we forget to do? That's right: We forget how to breathe, and we suddenly become shallow breathers. When this happens, pause for a moment, smile contemplatively, and take a deep breath or two. Chances are you will remember what comes next in your presentation, and you can carry on. If not, be honest with the audience and say, "I just had a brain cloud and forgot what I was about to say." The audience won't turn on you because you just showed them that you are a human being and even you, the person on the stage, can make a mistake.

As speakers, presenters, and facilitators, we need to be very cognizant of our breathing and the effect it is having on our voice. Breathing is one of the most critical components in public speaking and it is one of the least taught subjects. Think of it this way, you may be the subject matter expert, but if your voice can't command an audience and keep them engaged, then the audience can't act on your words.

Breathing is one of the most critical components in public speaking and it is one of the least taught subjects.

With a strong, powerful, and confident voice, you will influence people's lives, so practice your breathing. Inhale and expand your diaphragm. Exhale slowly and squeeze all the air out.

Takeaways

- Do deep breathing exercises every day so you can deliver your thoughts and ideas without falling flat.
- Take it slow so you can build up your stamina.
- With a strong, powerful, and confident voice, you will influence people's lives

The Importance of Nonverbal Communication — Yours and Theirs

"When the eyes say one thing, and the tongue another, a practiced man relies on the language of the first."

— Ralph Waldo Emerson

Nonverbal communication is something most of us don't think about often, but we should. In fact, I think it is something that should be at the forefront of your mind as you prepare your presentation. Nonverbal communication is sending wordless clues to your audience and receiving the messages they send back to you. These clues include body language, distance and space, physical environments, tone of your voice, and touch. Approximately two-thirds of all communication is nonverbal. Think about it: the way you listen, look and move; the position of your body; and tone of your voice all work together to inform the other person's perception of you. Based on this perception, they decide whether you care or not, whether you are a credible storyteller or a deceptive one, and those judgments can significantly impact whether they listen attentively or dismiss your words.

Nonverbal communication is a two-way street — you are on one side of the road, and your audience is on the other. To better connect and more efficiently communicate with an audience, all presenters need to spend time learning to read body language and nonverbal clues. You need to study your clues, and also those sent back to you by the audience. Like everything else in building strong presentation skills, nonverbal communication is an acquired skill honed through practice and repetition.

Let's start with the messages an audience may send to *you* through their body language.

To better connect and more efficiently communicate with an audience, all presenters need to spend time learning to read body language and nonverbal clues.

If many in your audience are looking at their phones, slouched in their seats and not making eye contact with you, they are disengaged. What about the crossed-arms body position? That is a defensive position that may mean you said something to upset the audience. Another nonverbal sign that I look for is the deer-in-the-headlights look, which means they quit listening to you a while ago. If, however, just a *few* people sit with their arms crossed, they are either comfortable sitting this way or the room is very cold! Stay vigilant and attentive to audience reactions so you can tell whether your people are with you or drifting off.

When you are aware of your audience's body language, you can react quickly and seamlessly to re-engage them. A quick five-minute break can work, especially during long presentations or workshops. It's difficult to stay involved with a presenter when you desperately need a seventh-inning stretch. If the information that you are presenting is loaded with statistics, data, facts, and figures, it can be difficult to keep an audience's attention — dry material is, well, dry. Remember that a great way to engage that audience is to touch their emotions through a *story* that illustrates the value of all those numbers.

I believe the most challenging part of analyzing nonverbal communication is being cognizant of your own. You put in countless hours of preparation developing, writing, and practicing your presentation leading up to the big day. All that hard work can be for naught the moment you step in front of the audience if your nonverbal communication is incongruent with the words you choose.

Think about a time when you delivered a presentation and you were not adequately prepared or didn't have the in-depth knowledge necessary to feel confident. I bet your voice was shaky and cracked, your arms were held close to your body, probably around your abdomen area, maybe your fists were clenched. In a case like this, the nonverbal clues sent to your audience say loudly and clearly that you are not the subject-matter expert and you are not confident in the presentation.

Colin Blalock, CPA, has spent time teaching himself the art of nonverbal communication after reading *Telling Lies* by Dr. Paul Ekman.[23] I have known Colin for many years and I once asked him to do me a favor at a conference where I was speaking and he was attending. I asked him to analyze my body language during this presentation and give me some feedback. Luckily, he agreed. I must admit ... I was a little nervous to receive his feedback.

After the presentation, Colin told me that I came across as very honest and open. That was just the sort of feedback I had hoped for. He told me that my nonverbal body language was something called the "Truth Plane." The way he described it, when your hands are out in front of you, elbows about waist high, with palms up, the audience will perceive you are telling the truth and that you are passionate about your topic.

Mark Bowden, an expert in human behavior, delivered a speech on the "Truth Plane" at a TEDx conference in Toronto.[24] He started his speech by pausing and holding his arms out with his palms up between his midsection and his heart. Through his nonverbal communication, he already signaled to the audience that what they were going to hear would be the truth, and that he was very passionate about the topic.

---

23   Eckman, Paul, *Telling Lies: Clues to Deceit in the Marketplace, Politics, and Marriage*, W. W. Norton & Company; Revised edition (January 26, 2009).

24   Bowden, Mark, "Truth Plane" TedX Talk, http://truthplane.com/.

Watch a video recording of your presentation and do so with the sound *off* so you can look closely at your body gestures. What are your hands doing? What messages are your facial expressions transmitting to your audience?

There are two ways you can assess your body language on stage. One way is to hire Colin Blalock to watch your presentation and provide you with feedback. Probably not the most practical option but a good one.

➤   You can listen to my interview with Colin by going to my website, PeterMargaritis.com, clicking on the "Improv Is No Joke" podcast icon, and going to episode 77.

Another way is to video your presentation then watch it with a critical eye. First, watch it with no sound and look closely at your body gestures. What are your hands doing? What messages are your facial expressions transmitting to your audience? After viewing it a few times with the sound off, turn the sound on so you can evaluate the sound of your voice and see your body language in a new way. Listen and watch to see if your words are congruent with your nonverbal clues. Recruit a trusted colleague to watch your video so they can offer their feedback, too.

Improving nonverbal communication is nothing new. There is plenty of research on this topic dating as far back as Charles Darwin. Take the time to learn more so you can improve your nonverbal skills. I recommend Dr. Ekman's two popular books *Emotions Revealed* and

Telling Lies.[25] His work has helped both national and regional law enforcement in their work, and his research was the inspiration for the award-winning television series *Lie to Me.*

There are many resources available to help you learn more about reading an audience's nonverbal clues. Your success as a presenter is, in great part, contingent on being able to send out the nonverbal messages you want your audience to receive, and to watch your audience for their feedback. Develop those skills by using them every day, in every interaction, whether with co-workers, friends, or family. You'll be amazed at what you learn.

Takeaways

- Think about how your non-verbal communication looks to your audience.

- When you are passionate about your subject, it will be demonstrated in your "Truth Plane."

- Record your next presentation, turn down the sound, and watch your non-verbal communication.

---

25   Ekman PhD, Paul, *Emotions Revealed: Recognizing Faces and Feelings to Improve Communication and Emotional Life*, 2nd Edition, Holt Paperbacks; 2nd edition, 2007.

Section 3
CASE STUDIES

CASE STUDY #1

ARIZONA SOCIETY OF CPAS ACCOUNTING AND AUDITING PRESENTATION

I was presenting an Accounting and Auditing Update at the Arizona Society of CPAs Accounting and Reporting Standards Conference. The night before the presentation, I was reviewing my slides, and thinking about consolidations of variable interest entities (VIE) — one of the topics I would be discussing the next day. Consolidation of VIEs is a highly sophisticated accounting standard that the profession has been struggling with ever since the Enron scandal.

According to Investopedia, a variable interest entity "is an entity that an investor has a controlling interest in, but this controlling interest is not based on a majority of voting rights. VIEs are subject to consolidation under certain conditions."[26] The consolidation of variable interest entities is not a strategy that companies want to take because it can increase the overall debt position of an organization's balance sheet. The approach most organizations want to make is to keep these VIEs off the balance sheet.

---

26   Investopedia, "Noncontrolling Interest," https://www.investopedia.com/terms/n/noncontrolling_interest.asp.

Have I put you to sleep yet?
Hang in there with me.

As I was reviewing this material, I could envision the audience getting extraordinarily bored and either sleepy or pulling out their cell phones to begin what is known as the "conference prayer." The conference prayer is when a speaker looks out at their audience and feels as if they're on a pulpit instead of a stage because all the audience members have their heads bowed like they're in prayer (because they're reading their email or checking social media).

Having spoken at this conference in the past, I had a good idea of the demographics of this audience. It consisted of sole practitioners, and employees of small- to medium-size businesses with only a few large accounting firms or corporations with people in attendance. The audience needed to understand this information at a 50,000-foot level and not at the extreme detail that I was planning. Now, the challenge became how to present this information in a manner that everyone in the audience could understand.

I began asking myself what the lowest common denominator would be in the situation. In other words, what were the standard-setters trying to accomplish with this proposed rule? Then it dawned on me ... they were trying to move an entity into another entity but the entity didn't want it to move in. And through this thought process, I had my "aha" moment.

The next day when I got to the title slide that read "consolidations of variable interest entities," I saw the audience react in the way that I was anticipating, beginning the process of the conference prayer. I addressed the audience by saying, "I would just like to take a moment and get to know you all just a little bit better. By a show of hands, how many of you are married?" I got some interesting looks to this question, but out of the more than 200 attendees, approximately 80% raise their hand. Then I asked, "How many of you have a mother-in-law?" All the hands remain raised. A few people snickered.

I then said, "I want you to think of your mother-in-law as a variable interest entity." At this point, a picture of an older woman appeared on the screen and underneath the picture were the letters VIE. Then I said, "Your spouse wants their mother to move into your household, but you do not want your mother-in-law moving in (also known as *consolidating*) into your household."

What I witnessed from the audience was what I was hoping to see. The audience went from preparing to disengage from the presentation to be entirely focused on the presentation and laughing at the analogy. They were smiling. This was going to go well.

I paused for a moment. Next on the screen three pictures appeared and I said, "Your mother-in-law receives money from Social Security, a retirement account, and she loves to play the slot machines." The audience was engaged entirely and not even thinking about looking at their cell phones.

Next to appear on the screen was a picture of the six children from the Brady Bunch. I said, "Your mother-in-law has six children, and they all contribute to the financial well-being of their mother. However, your family contributes the most on a percentage basis because your spouse is a principal at a high school and loves to be in control." (At this point a picture of a nameplate that said principal appeared on the screen.)

Then I said, "Let's recap. Your spouse wants their VIE mother to consolidate onto your balance sheet because your spouse is the principal in this arrangement. However, you prefer to have your VIE mother-in-law *not* consolidate onto your balance sheet. You prefer that she spend two months with each of her children (you know — her agents) so no one has to have her consolidate onto their balance sheet."

I know that I have a pretty cool and memorable last name, but when I go back to the Arizona Society CPAs to speak, someone will always come up to me and say, "You're the mother-in-law guy, right?" That's when I know I did my job by taking very complex accounting information and having presented it in a manner that everyone could understand. Entertainment and humor are what the audience craves to help keep them engaged in the presentation.

This example is a form of storytelling. The villain was the complexity of a variable interest entity and, because of the complexity surrounding the data, the high probability that the audience would disengage from the presentation. The hero was the ability to create a story around the complex information and put it in a context that was relatable to everyone.

On a side note, I knew that I was taking on some risk here in presenting this information in the manner that I did. Just before I got to the slide about consolidations of variable interest entities, I almost chickened out. I thought that if this bombed, I would never be asked to speak for this association again. Then I thought if this is a home run, I will achieve the goal of keeping the audience engaged along with increasing the level of retention around this material. As they say in improv, follow the fear.

CASE STUDY #2

STEVE FORBES' ECONOMIC UPDATE SPEECH

National Speakers Association Annual Convention
San Diego, California

I was attending the National Speakers Association Annual Convention in 2014 when I heard the most incredible economic update speech. Most economic update speeches are done by economists who work with major financial institutions. These speeches can be incredibly dry, boring, and uninspiring.

Let me share with you the demographics of the National Speakers Association audience. There were 1,500 attendees that year; roughly 85% were right brainers, about 10% would be considered accounting and finance types, mostly Baby Boomers and early Gen Xers, all entrepreneurs and small businesses with a variety of cultures being represented. We were in one of the hotel's large ballrooms, with the lights dimmed down in the audience and bright lights at the stage.

We kick off our convention on a Sunday afternoon with a high-powered, high-energy, highly motivating and theatrical opening. As I was reviewing the agenda, I noticed that Steve Forbes was going to deliver an economic update right after the opening. My first thought was he was going to put everyone to sleep because to go from a highly energetic opening to the exact opposite of an economic update is like going 100 miles an hour and now slamming on your brakes. I had envisioned the audience, within about five minutes of him taking the stage, either going to sleep, walking out, or beginning the conference prayer. Let's just say I was completely and happily wrong.

Mr. Forbes understands Albert Einstein's concept, "If you can't explain it simply, you don't know it." He began speaking from behind the podium and was not using PowerPoint, which I applaud. What I witnessed for 45 minutes was one of the best financial story-tellers in the world. He used humor and put things in a context that everybody in the room could relate to.

Here is a brief piece from his speech:

> *"I mentioned monetary policy earlier and gave you the warning.*
> *The thing about money, the thing to remember about money,*
> *which the Federal Reserve (our central bank) does not realize, is*
> *that money is simply a means to make it easier to buy and sell with*
> *each other. It makes transactions easier. In the old days we had*
> *barter ... let's say I wanted to buy an iPad 2,000 years ago. So I go*
> *to the Apple store with my herd of goats and the store owner says*
> *he doesn't want goats — he wants sheep. I try to figure out how*
> *to swap goats for sheep and our sheep herder makes sure wolves*
> *don't eat the sheep. The sheep herder wants to be paid in red wine.*
> *I have white wine so it just becomes very cumbersome. [Laughs.]*
> *Imagine that we had barter today. Imagine trying to deposit*
> *a cow in an ATM."*

Clearly, he did his homework and knew his audience well. He didn't use highly technical economic terms except for a brief mention of monetary policy. But he then put it in terms that everybody could understand and just used the word money. And then you crafted stories that put his points into contexts that everybody in the audience could relate to.

Mr. Forbes nailed this economic update and got a standing ovation from the crowd. To this day, I have never ever seen anyone give an economic update and receive a standing ovation except for Mr. Forbes.

In looking back on why that presentation was so strong, I can see he had a winning formula. He did three things that are key in delivering a powerful financial presentation. First, he knew his audience. Second, he tailored his speech to this audience. Finally, he did not use economic jargon, or buzzwords — he put highly technical language into a context that everyone in that audience could relate to. He told stories and jokes and shared relatable analogies.

The next time you are delivering any type of presentation about a complex technical topic, spend time thinking about who was sitting in that audience and put things in context or analogies that everyone can relate to.

Yes, this will take a lot of hard work and no, you are not dumbing down the content. You are crafting your presentation so that everyone in your audience can understand the topic much better. This hard work will pay off tenfold and your audience will walk away with some much-needed knowledge that they can retain.

CASE STUDY #3

EXPLAINING PROFITABILITY WITH A DOLLAR BILL

When I worked at the Victoria's Secret Catalogue (VSC) headquarters, there was a quarterly all-company meeting led by the CEO of Limited Brands (parent of VSC). The purpose of the meeting was to share the organization's business outlook with all employees. When it was the CFO's turn to speak about company profitability, you could immediately see people glazing over like a Krispy Kreme donut. This was way before the greatest invention to combat boring technical presentations: the smartphone. The audience had to endure the torture, escaping only as far as our imaginations could take us.

Because this was an all-company meeting, those in the audience were from every department: human resources, sales, customer service, marketing, accounting, and IT. In this case (and many like it), the CFO did not translate technical accounting and financial information in a way that the audience could understand. In other words, he was trying to explain the organization income statement using accounting jargon and not plain English even though his audience represented various different types of functional expertise. He did not put the numbers and the information into a context that the audience could relate to. I'm sure many of you have experienced the same phenomenon wherever you work. As a technical presenter, that CFO did not consider his audience and never stepped into the shoes of our audience.

Over the years, many accounting and financial professionals have told me versions of the same story. They recognized the problem — people were not engaged in the presentation. But they didn't know how to correct it. My advice to them was to deliver the information in a way that everyone could relate to.

To better explain this point, I have created a real-life example: the Delta Air Lines 2016 income statement. Delta reported almost $40 billion in revenue with $33 billion in operating expenses and a net profit of $4 billion. I have never seen, let alone touched, $1 billion, and $40 billion blows my mind. Have you ever seen that much money? (Probably not, but if you have, please contact me directly because I am always looking for investors!) For most of us, a billion of anything is difficult to imagine. So you need to ask yourself what can everyone in your audience relate to? DING, a single dollar bill! Right? Everybody knows what a $1 bill looks and feels like. They can relate.

Now let's use a single dollar bill to explain the profitability of Delta Air Lines. In order to do that, we need to common size the income statement. Investopedia defines and describes a common size income statement as "an income statement in which each account is expressed as a percentage of the value of sales. It is used for vertical analysis, in which each line item in a financial statement is listed as a percentage of a base figure within the statement, to make comparisons easier."[27]

---

27   Investopedia, "Common Size Income Statement," https://www.investopedia.com/terms/c/commonsizeincomestatement.asp#ixzz5K1vfWBjH.

If I were the CFO at Delta Airlines presenting to a diverse audience, I would begin the presentation by showing a one-dollar bill on a PowerPoint slide. I'd open with, "This is how we spent every dollar our passengers paid us for flying with our airline this past year." The single dollar bill represents the $40 billion in total revenue. Next, I would move the focus to the expenses, beginning with the largest single expense then work my way down the income statement. I would continue my conversation by saying, "$0.22 of every dollar goes to cover payroll, your salaries (at this point, 22% of the dollar is covered up – see illustration below). After that, $0.17 of every dollar goes to cover fuel costs. As we all know, fuel costs can fluctuate on a daily basis, no different from your automobile fuel costs. $0.10 of every dollar goes to pay our regional carriers. This year, $0.07 went to pay taxes because we had a profitable year. The remaining expenses grouped together (profit sharing, maintenance costs, utilities, etc.) totaled $0.33. After all this is said and done, we got to keep $0.11 from every dollar that our customers paid us for the privilege of flying Delta."

Below is a picture of how I might illustrate this on a PowerPoint slide.

DELTA AIRLINES

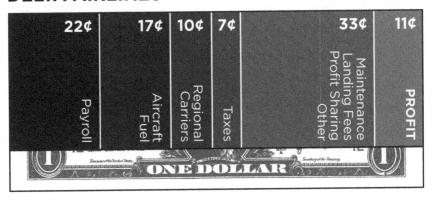

Now here's how we can turn this translated financial information into action. The audience in this case might look at the graphic and wonder what it would take to make that $0.22 of payroll larger. Fair enough, let's address the issue head on. I would say, "I know what you are all thinking. You would like to see that $0.22 of payroll grow larger to support bigger salaries and wages. To do this, we have to control other expenses better so we can become more profitable and put more money in your pockets."

"Let's look at those costs that are in the $0.33 category. I mentioned that utility costs are part of this group. Now, I'm going to sound like your dad when you were younger but please shut off the lights, computers, and other electronic devices plugged into Delta and help us lower our utility costs. Each one of you can do your small part in controlling utility costs that will have a positive effect on the overall profitability of our company. I cannot guarantee that doing this will lead to greater wages in the future, but what I will tell you is that it does increase the possibility of this happening."

Now you have empowered your workforce to have a direct impact on the financial position of your organization just by doing the simple task of turning off electricity when they are not using it. You can take a complex financial statement, make it easy to relate to, and give your employees the opportunity to directly impact the profitability of your company. That's a powerful message that everyone can relate to.

CASE STUDY #4
FIVE NINES TECHNOLOGY GROUP

Lincoln, NE
GoNines.com

I delivered a half-day seminar to 30 members of the Nebraska Society of CPAs titled *Financial Storytelling: The Key to Growing Your Organization to the Next level.* The next day, I received the following email from Jennie Scheel, CFO of Five Nines Technology Group:

> *"After your session, I know I could make significant improvements to my quarterly presentation to the staff. I am going to run the breakdown of a dollar past the owners, as I think that's an excellent way to tell the story to our employees!*
>
> *Each month I provide the owners with many spreadsheets, graphs, and a summary email of the month. Prior to this session, I have been thinking about how to present this information in a 1-page executive summary instead of the huge amount of data I provide every month! We are a privately held company, with 2 owners, so the report would be going just to them, along with the President.*
>
> *Have you seen any great summaries that are provided that tell the story on 1 page each month? I am trying to envision the best way to tell the story to IT guys [both owners were competing IT guys then joined together to build a company] and thought I'd ask if you had any recommendations to get started.*

Again, I really appreciate all the information you shared today. After this session, I'm motivated to get better connected with the audience at all staff meetings, along with monthly reporting to the owners."

Five Nines is an information technology company that provides managed IT services to the healthcare, financial, legal, and professional services industries.

Internal Reporting

Each month, Jennie sends a financial package to the owners, which includes the balance sheet, cash flow statement, and working capital report, along with a summary email. However, in her words, she states, "clearly I overwhelm them with my spreadsheets and data."

On a quarterly basis, Jennie presents this financial information to the entire staff. She includes information that she thinks is necessary concerning the investment in employee benefits that exceed industry standards (such as providing better healthcare coverage at a lower monthly cost to employees, company matching of 401[k] contributions, etc.). Most organizations don't exceed industry standards, but the information seems to fall on deaf ears. Why?

I requested that Jennie email me the last quarterly report. When I opened the file, it was like an avalanche of numbers that poured out of my computer and buried me alive. Jennie and I started a conversation about reducing the volume of information down to something that is quick and easy, so the organization can get a snapshot understanding of the business.

The area that she wanted to work on the most was how to deliver her financial information in a manner that the audience would appreciate and understand. She agreed to reduce the amount of information to a few key points on her PowerPoint slides, and to incorporate the dollar bill strategy discussed in Case Study #3. I inquired about how senior management was dressed for this presentation and what the dress code was for the rest of the organization. Should senior management change to a more casual style to better connect with everyone else?

So, the senior management team started dressing in "business casual" from their normal "business formal" attire. This small change had an immediate effect on senior management's ability to connect with its team. The new perception was that senior management was communicating at the level of everyone, versus a top-down approach. They removed some of the hierarchy.

In preparation for her first quarterly financial report to the organization, Jennie kept thinking, more pictures and less data. The dollar bill strategy that I shared in the prior case really resonated with her and motivated her to find a different way.

Jennie took a risk and changed the way she delivered her financial information, which was a success, as evidenced by her email follow-up below. By reducing the amount of financial information, she delivered only what was pertinent to the audience, moved away from accounting jargon, and put the information into contexts to which the entire audience could relate. She created stronger connections that ultimately led to a better financial understanding by everyone. This is the goal of the CFO, right?

She emailed me the day after the presentation saying:

"Just finished my all-staff presentation. I have received a huge number of compliments on the breakdown of the dollar bill! I attached my version of the dollar bill, Five Nines style!

Thanks again for your amazing coaching, which allowed me to give a presentation during which everyone kept their heads up and didn't go into the presentation prayer mode."

CASE STUDY #5

DELEON & STANG, CPAS AND ADVISORS

Gaithersburg, MD
DeLeonAndStang.com

DeLeon & Stang is one of the most progressive accounting firms in Maryland, if not the entire United States. Their philosophy and strategy are spot-on and have evolved over the life of the firm. They have entirely grasped the full meaning of the "firm of the future" and the anticipatory CPA. If you are not sure what this means, ask Google.

The firm was founded more than 30 years ago by Allen DeLeon and Richard Stang. Both Allen and Richard did not grow up in traditional public accounting firms. They were working for the American Trucking Association and doing taxes on the side. Allen and Rich not starting their careers in public accounting has a lot to do with the culture and attitudes within the firm.

Both see the business of public accounting in a very different light. That light is because Allen and Rich understand that the business they are in is the *people* business first and everything else is a by-product of that. Without people, they have no business.

This story fits nicely into this book, at a different angle, because it is about building relationships and understanding that tapping into one's emotions increases productivity, increases retention, and ultimately increases profitability.

First let me share some background on the firm, taken from their website.

Firm Profile

"For over 30 years DeLeon & Stang, Certified Public Accountants and Advisors, has been one of the Mid-Atlantic's premier accounting firms. We provide the highest quality accounting, tax, audit, advisory, financial, business and professional services to both individuals and organizations.

Our clients like our friendly, no-nonsense style. Our understanding of their industries and problems enables us to successfully advise them, helping them keep their businesses alive and strong. Our staff are trained experts; clients can come to us for solutions that make sense. You can count on us to tell it to you straight — with integrity, trust, and innovation."

Partners:
- Allen DeLeon
- Richard Stang
- Jeanie Price
- Brad Hoffman
- Dan Dellon

Mission Statement, Core Value, and How We Serve

Improving the lives of our staff, clients, and community with innovation, trust and integrity.

Core Values:
- Putting our people first
- Being on the leading edge
- Thinking tomorrow, Now!
- Improving continuously
- Delivering the client WOW factor

How We Serve:
- Teamwork
- Passion
- Innovation
- Flexibility
- Communication

What makes DeLeon & Stang unique is demonstrated in their order of priorities in their mission statement. Staff comes first before clients. Before this revision, clients were listed before staff, although they have operated for more than 30 years in just the opposite manner.

Their hiring practices and retention strategy help to serve their clients at the highest level. For example, they provide their staff with unlimited PTO and no mandatory Saturdays during busy seasons. This attitude demonstrates that the partners trust that their team will service the client needs, first, before serving their needs. Entirely different from most public accounting firms that I have seen.

The following is from an interview that I conducted with one of the firm's partners, Brad Hoffman, to get a more in-depth understanding of why they are so unique. Here are some of the critical points that Brad makes during the interview.

Brad:

When I meet with a client, let's say for an hour, we talk about the numbers for maybe 10 to 15 minutes, tops. The rest of the time we talk about where your business is going, how you are doing, what makes you happy and what are your goals. These clients went into business because they were either good at it or had a passion for it. The ability to relate to their mindset helps in understanding their emotional state. By doing so, there is a higher trust content and you can build off the things they want to do in life.

Peter:

[I share a story with Brad about a friend of mine who works in public accounting who personally delivered a tax return to her client because it was on the way to her house.] When she showed up, the client was surprised because nobody from the firm came out to visit her and her business. The client gave my friend a three-hour tour of her business. The next day, she told the partners about her experience, and they replied: "You are billing her for your time." My friend no longer works for the firm.

Brad:

We do accounting assessments where we go out to a client and assess their accounting systems and provide them with a report on how their firm can help make their accounting department better. The person who runs the assessment team is excellent at delineating processes and is very narrative. In preparation to deliver the report to the client, we printed out the six-page document, which contained lots of data, facts, and figures. This printing magnified the problem because as a business owner, I would never sit down and read this document. We needed to condense this into a concise bullet-point document so that the owner would take the time to review our comments.

After we sent this information, we received an email that was emotionally driven by our short document. The client's email said, "I love this s$%t! When do we start?" It's about knowing the client, who is the human behind the business. If you treat all your clients the same, you are only making some of them happy.

Peter:

When you meet a new prospect, how do you answer this question, "Tell me about your firm?" How do you explain who you are and what makes you different?

Brad:

I don't. I ask them about their business first. They don't want to know about my firm at first. Tell me if you have ever met a business owner that didn't want to tell you about their business? Why did they get in this business? My goal is to learn more about them so I can provoke the emotion of care, concern, and interest.

Have you ever heard of a client saying, "I love going to the accountant's office?" We have clients who enjoy their trip to our office. I have a client who relocated to North Carolina and they come back every year for their sit-down meeting with us. We create an experience for our clients because we care what is going on in their lives. We understand that we deliver a service, not just a product.

I use the "well if it did work, what would it look like" approach. when a client says "that process won't work." I follow up with "well if it did work, what would it look like?" This will frustrate some clients, but they will come back at some point and say "you made me think about the issue in greater detail and that's what I needed to do."

I like to build a positive emotional experience around interactions with people. That is what they will remember.

DeLeon & Stang is a unique accounting firm where the people understand that it is more than a 1040, 1120, or an audit. It is about creating a *relationship* with their clients, providing them with a solid product, and genuinely caring about the wellbeing of the organizations they serve and the lives those organizations impact in turn. If I were a member of this firm and someone asked me the question, "tell me about your firm," I would respond, very much as they already, expertly do: "We are in the people business because we care about the lives of our staff and clients. Please tell me more about *your* organization."

CONCLUSION

I hope this book has given you ideas on how you can better explain and present financial information to those who are non-accountants and to younger accountants to help to increase their knowledge quicker. Please always remember that the size of the audience doesn't matter when you are trying to connect with them. One person or 1,000 people — every audience is an important audience. Also, remember, it is not about you; it is all about your audience. To put some of the lessons of this book to use in your work, you will have to work a little harder at first. But if you use the techniques that I have described, over time, this will become second nature to you.

If you are reading this and thinking, "I can never do half the stuff that is written in this book," I'd reminder you of the question DeLeon & Stang partner Brad Hoffman likes to ask his clients. Ask yourself: "Well, if it *did* work, what would it look like?" Imagine implementing the lessons in this book and truly excelling at that. What would it look like? Write down the answer.

For example, it's easy to that that you don't have the time to develop your slides — one slide, one picture, and one thought per slide. But what if you *did* make the time? Well, if it *did* work, what would that look like? It would look like:

- The audience is more focused and listening to me
- The audience is not in the conference prayer mode

- I can tell that the audience is understanding the material based off their body language.

This technique that Brad uses is very similar to the improv technique of "Yes! And ..."

- Yes, I can use the technique of one slide, one picture, and one thought AND the audience won't be bored to death.

- Yes, I can use the technique of one slide, one picture, and one thought AND I won't have to look at everyone with their head bowed and reading their email.

- Yes, I can use the technique of one slide, one picture, and one thought AND I will be successful in delivering my message.

It all comes down to your attitude and desire to become better and there are two places to start. First, join a local Toastmasters club and work on your delivery. Second, join the National Speakers Association (nsaspeaker.org) and learn about the speaking profession. Find your local chapter and go to a meeting to test-drive the organization. There are CPAs, accountants, and financial professionals who are members of NSA — I assure you that I'm not the only one, and that you'll be among friends! In my tenure with NSA, my overall speaking persona is so much stronger than ever and it keeps evolving.

My business today is focused on helping CPAs, accountants, and financial professionals to become stronger presenters and facilitators. I speak at conferences and seminars on this topic and on the topic of Improv Is No Joke. I love getting my audiences to see that improv is more than just being funny — it's a way to grow your career and your business.

I wish you all the best success and I thank you for reading. If I can help you in any way, please send me an email at Peter@PeterMargaritis.com or connect in any of the various ways listed below.

Learn more about the book, and quickly link to all the social media channels:
TakingTheNumbOutOfNumbersBook.com

Send an email:
Peter@PeterMargaritis.com

Hire Peter for keynotes and workshops for CPA and financial professional associations (chapter, regional, national):
PeterMargaritis.com

Read Peter's previous book, available on Amazon in paperback and Kindle editions:
Improv Is No Joke: Using Improvisation to Create Positive Results in Leadership and in Life

Listen to the podcast:
Change Your Mindset with Peter A. Margaritis, CPA

Find, follow and share on social media:
Facebook.com/TheAccidentalAccountant
Twitter.com/PMargaritis
LinkedIn.com/in/PeterMargaritis/

ACKNOWLEDGMENTS

There are so many people who I want to thank, and I will. But I would be remiss if I didn't start off by thanking **Pam Devine and Tom Hood at The Maryland Association of CPAs and The Business Learning Institute**. In the summer of 2016, a prospect contacted Pam to see if they had a course on financial storytelling. There was none. Then I got a call from Pam asking if I could and would develop this course. I answered with a resounding "YES! And ... this will be fun." To date, I have delivered *Financial Storytelling: Taking Your Organization to the Next Level* more than 20 times. That course is now titled (you guessed it!) *Taking the Numb Out of Numbers*.

Interestingly, the title was the hardest part in writing this book. I mulled over it for months, kicking around a variety of ideas but not really liking any of them. In January 2018, at a National Speakers Association Ohio Chapter meeting, about 10 of us were discussing our businesses with our guest speaker. I made the comment that I was really struggling coming up with a title for this book. After I explained the premise of the book, **Maureen Zappala**, President of the Chapter, said "What about *Taking the Numb Out of Numbers*?" just off the cuff. Thank you, Maureen!

Then I took the title and pitched it at speaking events or anytime I was in front of CPAs, accountants, and other financial professionals. Some of them replied, "if you take the *numb* out of the numbers, all you have left is just 'ers.'" It was said so many times that I said to myself, I need to create the acronym E.R.S. I had a Zoom call with **Bret Johnson at the Association of International Certified Professional Accountants (AICPA)** and told him this story. He paused for a second, had this weird look in his eye, and said "E.R.S stands for Effective Relatable Stories." WOW – I wish I had that talent. Thanks, Bret!

For all she has done to help me write this book, I would like to thank **Cathy Fyock, The Biz Book Strategist,** who is my book coach and who gave me the motivation to keep plugging ahead. Her monthly webinars and coaching calls were the exact pieces I needed during this past year. Also a big thanks to **Claudia Trusty of Trusty and Company** who took my words, edited them, and made me sound better. I do believe that she went through gallons of red ink in her editing. I want to thank **Karl Ahlrich, Merle Heckman, and Cathy Fyock** (again) for being on my editorial board and providing me with feedback on how to make the book better.

The cover of my book was designed by **Tom Trusty of Trusty and Company** and he used his creative wizardry and developed an eye-catching cover. Tom and Claudia have been my web designers, webmasters, and marketing consultants for more than 15 years. More than that, they have been close and dear friends for over 20 years. Thanks again, Tom and Claudia.

The foreword of this book was written by a good friend — **Boyd Search, the CEO of the Georgia Society of CPAs**. Boyd was the VP of Education at the Ohio Society of CPAs prior to his departure in 2010. Over the years, Boyd has been a great supporter of my business, as I have been of his. On his first day at the GSCPA, I became his first new member and have maintained my membership ever since. He also purchased 40 copies of my previous book, *Improv is No Joke*, to give to his board and staff. In the speaking world, Boyd has known me the longest and was the no-brainer choice to write the foreword. Thanks, Boyd!

I'd like to thank **Kate Colbert, Courtney Hudson, and the entire team at Silver Tree Publishing** for turning a manuscript and a dream into a book. Kate's business model and approach to publishing business books is all about providing a greater revenue stream for her authors, which, in and of itself, tells you a lot about her character. She has made this process as painless as possible for me, and I'm left thoroughly believing she can survive on only a few hours of sleep. Now that the book is finished, we can all rest! Thank you, Kate!

I would like to thank **Jennie Scheel, CFO at FiveNines Technology Group**, for her enthusiasm and time as we transformed the way she delivers financial information to her company. Also, a heartfelt thanks for allowing that story to be included in the book. Thanks, Jennie!

I would like to thank **Brad Hoffman, a partner in the accounting firm of DeLeon & Stang**, for giving me the gift of his time to discuss how their progressive, future-ready firm has positioned itself to meet the needs of staff, clients, and the community. They are a very forward-thinking firm that is building a sustainable business. I'm grateful to DeLeon & Stang for allowing me to include that story in the book. Thanks Brad! Also, I would like to thank **Rich Stang** for taking time out of his schedule to be interviewed, along with Brad for an episode on my podcast that discusses in depth their case study in the book. Thanks, Rich, and thank you to the other partners as well — **Allen DeLeon, Jeanie Price, and Dan Dellon!**

I would like to thank **Tom Hood, Jack Park, Clarke Price, Kristen Rampe, Jennifer Elder, Ashley Matthews, Byron Patrick, Hayden Williams, Amy Vetter, and Bob Dean** for taking the time to pre-read my book and provide me with a testimonial. Greatly appreciated and thank you!

A special thank you goes to **the National Speakers Association and to the Ohio Chapter.** The spirit of NSA, which is built around the ideas of mutual support, shared success, and giving back, has been instrumental to me in becoming a better presenter, facilitator, and entrepreneur.

I want to thank **my mother Pauline, brother Steve, sister Stacie, and brother-in-law Rick** for your love, compassion, and humor.

Finally, I want to thank **my wife, Mary, and my son, Stephen, and my two Labrador retrievers, Midnight and MJ**, for putting up with me during this process. Mary and Stephen, I could not have accomplished this without your love, support, and carefully placed humor and sarcasm, when I needed it the most. Midnight and MJ — your tails wagging always brings a smile

ABOUT THE AUTHOR

Peter A. Margaritis, CPA

Going from being a CPA to taking the "numb out of numbers" for thousands of other accountants is definitely the road less traveled, but that is exactly the path Peter Margaritis chose.

Accounting was never the career Peter envisioned for himself at 17 — standup comedy was going to be his ticket. However, based on his father's advice — "Don't be a funny guy, Pete. Be a CPA, you'll never be hungry." — and a knack for numbers, Peter earned his Master's in Accountancy and then his CPA license. He worked in key positions in several large organizations, and did very well. But accounting really wasn't his passion. He was, in fact, The Accidental Accountant.

During his time as a corporate CPA, Peter took improv classes and performed stand-up comedy. Communicating directly with audiences was life changing, and Peter discovered his true passion: Teaching what he knew rather than being a practicing CPA. That led him to university faculty positions where Peter combined his accounting skills with his improv performance skills. He realized his students not only learned more when they were entertained and engaged, they retained that knowledge and could apply it in new situations. It was an epiphany.

"Applied improv is all about the ability to draw upon your experience, knowledge and education to apply them in a way that meets the needs of the person you are taking to or working with – and it can be taught."

Peter decided to apply the lessons learned in his classrooms to help others in the accounting profession. Accountants face many inflexible situations filled with details, laws, rules, and deadlines. Improv, on the other hand, is very fluid, a concept that can be difficult to grasp without guidance and support. Peter helps bring the principles of improv to accountants who want to become more effective communicators and leaders. Yes, and he makes them laugh, learn, and grow.

Through his keynote presentations and customized workshops, Peter shows how the tools used in improv — like listening, flexibility, and trust — can change how a team interacts with each other and their clients. Bottom line, Peter help teams learn new methods to improve their communication and build stronger relationships with clients, customers, stakeholders, and associates.

Peter is a member of the Association for International Certified Professional Accountants (AICPA), Georgia Society of CPAs, Maryland Institute of CPAs, Ohio Society of CPAs and the National Speakers Association. He is past chair of the Ohio Society of CPAs and past delegate to the AICPA Board of Directors, and is currently the President of the Ohio Chapter of the National Speakers Association.

Peter lives in the Columbus, Ohio, area with his wife Mary and their son Stephen, and their two Labrador retrievers, Midnight and MJ.

Peter is an avid cyclist, cook and BBQer, humorist, improv virtuoso, and on a crusade to raise awareness of the signs of Type 1 diabetes in children. When he's not traveling for his business, he enjoys just hanging out with his family at home.

Taking the Numb Out of Numbers is Peter's second book.

🌐 **Learn more or connect with Peter:**
PeterMargaritis.com

✉️ **Mail or ship something special to:**
5606 Cypress Court
Westerville, OH 43082-7731

🎤 **To book Peter to speak:**
Visit PeterMargaritis.com/Contact/ and scroll down to "Book Peter to Speak" and fill out the contact form.

📕 **To order books in bulk and learn about quantity discounts:**
Send an email! Interested in ordering 10 or more copies of *Taking the Numb Out of Numbers* for your organization or association? Inquire at Peter@PeterMargaritis.com

REFERENCES

1. AICPA, Horizons 2025 Report, https://www.aicpa.org/ Research/CPAHorizons2025/DownloadableDocuments/ cpa-horizons-report-web.pdf.

2. *Ibid.*

3. The Maryland Association of Certified Public Accountants, Inc., and the Business Learning Institute, 2017, *Human Work in the Age of Machines: Five Steps for Building a Future Ready Finance Team* and *Human Work in the Age of Machines: Five Steps for Building a Future Ready Accounting Firm,* https://www.macpa. org/new-e-books-offer-steps-toward-future-readiness-for-cpas-f inance-professionals/.

4. Brown, Meta S., "He Turned Data Storytelling Success into Data Storytelling Failure; Here's What Went Wrong," *Forbes,* January 30, 2018, https://www.forbes.com/sites/meta-brown/2018/01/30/he-turned-data-storytelling-success-int o-data-storytelling-failure-heres-what-went-wrong/#2c1a106748a5.

5. Gallo, Carmine, *The Storyteller's Secret: From TED Speakers to Business Legends, Why Some Ideas Catch On and Others Don't,* (St. Martins Press, New York, 2016), 3.

6. *Ibid.*

7. Medina, John, *Brain Rules: 12 Principles for Surviving and Thriving at Work, Home and School*, (Pear Press, Seattle, WA, 2014) 112.

8. *Ibid.*

9. *Ibid.*

10. Mathews, Ryan D., and Wacker, Watts, *What's Your Story? Storytelling to Move Markets, Audiences, People, and Brands*, FT Press, 1st edition (August 30, 2007).

11. Austen, Hilary. "A Tale of Storytelling: Its Allure and Its Traps," *Harvard Business Review*, Case Study, 2014, https://hbr.org/product/a-tale-of-storytelling-its-allure-and-its-traps/ROT235-PDF-ENG.

12. Gottschall, Jonathan, "Theranos and the Dark Side of Storytelling," *Harvard Business Review*, Oct. 18, 2016, https://hbr.org/2016/10/theranos-and-the-dark-side-of-storytelling.

13. Carreyrou, John, "Hot Startup Theranos Has Struggled With Its Blood-Test Technology," *Wall Street Journal*, October 2015, https://www.wsj.com/articles/theranos-has-struggled-with-blood-tests-1444881901.

14. Bilton, Nick, "Exclusive: How Elizabeth Holmes's House of Cards Came Tumbling Down," *Vanity Fair*, September 2016, https://www.vanityfair.com/news/2016/09/elizabeth-holmes-theranos-exclusive.

15. TeachThought, "5 Quotes to Help Overcome the Fear of Public Speaking," August 29, 2017, https://www.teach-thought.com/technology/5-quotes-to-help-overcome-the-fear-of-public-speaking/.

16. Cuddy, Amy, "Your Body Language Shapes Who You Are," TEDGlobal 2012, June 2012, https://www.ted.com/talks/

amy_cuddy_your_body_language_shapes_who_you_are?refer-rer=playlist-the_most_popular_talks_of_all.

17. Piper, Watty, *The Little Engine That Could*, Philomel Books (September 27, 2005).

18. Washington, Megan, "Why I Live in Mortal Dread of Public Speaking," TEDxSydney 2014, April 2014, https://www.ted.com/talks/megan_washington_why_i_live_in_mortal_dread_of_public_speaking#t-19134.

19. Medina, John, *Brain Rules: 12 Principles for Surviving and Thriving at Work, Home and School*, (Pear Press, Seattle, WA, 2014), 182.

20. Reynolds, Garr, Top Ten Slide Tips, http://www.garrreynolds.com/preso-tips/design/.

21. Morgan, Nick, "How to Become an Authentic Speaker," *Harvard Business Review*, https://hbr.org/2008/11/how-to-become-an-authentic-speaker.

22. Shapira, Allison, "Breathing is the Key to Persuasive Public Speaking," *Harvard Business Review*, June 30, 2015, https://hbr.org/2015/06/breathing-is-the-key-to-persuasive-public-speaking.

23. Eckman, Paul, *Telling Lies: Clues to Deceit in the Marketplace, Politics, and Marriage*, W. W. Norton & Company; Revised edition (January 26, 2009).

24. Bowden, Mark, "Truth Plane" TedX Talk, http://truthplane.com/.

25. Ekman PhD, Paul, Emotions Revealed: Recognizing Faces and Feelings to Improve Communication and Emotional Life, 2nd Edition, Holt Paperbacks; 2nd edition, 2007.

26. Investopedia, "Noncontrolling Interest," https://www.investopedia.com/terms/n/noncontrolling_interest.asp.

27. Investopedia, "Common Size Income Statement," https://www.investopedia.com/terms/c/commonsizeincomestatement.asp#ixzz5K1vfWBjH.